Knitted Flowers

Knitted Flowers

30 SIMPLE FLORAL PATTERNS TO CREATE

Sian Brown

Contents

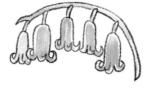

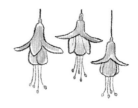

Introduction

Celebrate the seasons and brighten up your home with this colourful collection of knitted flowers. With 30 simple, easy-to-follow patterns and gorgeous colour photographs, even novice knitters will find they can quickly create beautiful blooms to enjoy throughout the year.

The flowers chosen for this book are well loved and will be a familiar sight in both gardens and the countryside. With a variety of flat and 3-D designs, they are mostly uncomplicated and quick to knit, and are ideal for using up small amounts of yarn left over from other knitting projects.

Knitted flowers can be used in a number of ways. As embellishments, sew them onto home knits such as throws and blankets, cushion covers and tea cosies, either individually or in groups. As trimmings for bags and hats they will provide an interesting detail and a seasonal look. Knitted flowers can be sewn onto garments, or made into brooches by adding a brooch pin to the back and used on jacket lapels for a quick wardrobe update. As ornaments, the flowers with stems can be put in vases, and the ones in pots displayed as they are. They could also be put into small garden or ceramic pots with decorative stones or fake earth.

So for a quick splash of colour year round, just pick up your needles and get knitting!

Sian

Anemone *Anemone coronaria*

A member of the buttercup family, anenomes are also called wind flowers, from the Greek name for wind (*anemos*), referring to the delicate petals being blown apart by the wind. They symbolize relaxation and anticipation as the flowers close at night and open during the day. Anemones are normally shades of pink, white, violet or red.

Materials

Small amounts of DK yarn in cerise (A), pink (B), cream (C), purple (D) and dark purple (E)

Pair of 3.75mm (UK9:US5) knitting needles

Tapestry needle

Finished size

5in (13cm) wide

Tip

The petals are knitted in one piece, working on a few stitches at a time. The centre is a rolled tab with embroidered French knots.

Pattern

Petals

Using C, cast on 15 sts, leaving a length of yarn.

K 2 rows.

Work on the first 3 sts as folls:

Row 1 (WS): P3.

Row 2: K1, m1, k1, m1, k1 (5 sts).

Row 3: K1, p to last st, k1.

Row 4: K1, m1, k to last st, m1, k1 (7 sts).

Change to B.

Row 5: P.

Row 6: K1, m1, k to last st, m1, k1 (9 sts).

Row 7: K1, p to last st, k1.

Row 8: K1, m1, k to last st, m1, k1 (11 sts).

St st 7 rows, keeping k1 at the beginning and end of the WS rows, change to A on row 10.

Row 16: K2tog, k to last 2 sts, k2tog (9 sts).

Row 17: K1, p to last st, k1.

Row 18: K2tog, k to last 2 sts, k2tog (7 sts).

Row 19: K1, p to last st, k1.

Row 20: K2tog, k to last 2 sts, k2tog (5 sts).

Row 21: K1, p to last st, k1.

Row 22: Cast off rem sts.

Cut the yarn and attach to the next st.

Rep until 5 petals have been made.

Centre (rolled tab)

Using D, cast on 15 sts.

K 1 row.

Cast off p wise.

To make up

Sew in the ends, leaving a length of yarn at the cast-on edge. Block and press the petals. Embroider in straight stitch (see page 139) above the colour change in the previous colour. Sew the bottom edges of the first and last petals together in A, thread the yarn through the cast-on edge, gather and secure. Using A, and with the petals slightly overlapping, secure one petal to the next on the lower section from the back.

Roll the centre and sew in the end. Take the yarn through to the opposite side a few times and secure. Using E, embroider French knots (see page 139) at the centre of the tab. Sew the finished tab onto the centre of the flower.

Bluebell *Hyacinthoides non-scripta*

Bluebells are spring-flowering plants often seen in woodlands, forming a dramatic colourful carpet when they are in bloom. The common name originates from the bell-like shape of the flowers and the colour, forming a delicate drooping shape.

Materials

Small amounts of 4-ply yarn in light blue (A) and dark green (B)

Pair of 3.25mm (UK10:US3) knitting needles

Pair of 3mm (UK11:US-) double-pointed knitting needles

Tapestry needle

Florist's wire

Finished size

5½in (14cm) long

Tip

The flowers are worked as a rectangle with a picot cast-off edge, which is gathered to form the shape.

Pattern

Flowers (make 8)
Using A and 3.25mm needles, cast on 11 sts.
St st 6 rows, starting with a k row.
Picot cast-off
Cast off 2 sts, * sl rem st on right-hand needle onto left-hand needle, cast on 2 sts, cast off 4 sts; rep from * to end, fasten off the remaining st, leaving a length of yarn.

Stem (make 2)
Using B and 3mm dpns, cast on 4 sts, leaving a length of yarn.
Make an i-cord 6¼in (16cm) long.
Cast off.

Small stems (make 6)
Using B and 3mm dpns, cast on 4 sts.
Make an i-cord 1¼in (3.5cm) long.
Cast off, leaving a length of yarn.

To make up
Sew the side seam of the flowers, starting at the cast-off edge. Leave a length of yarn. Thread the yarn around the cast-off edge and gather, leaving a small gap. Place one end of the i-cord for the main stem inside the flower, gather the edge and pull through a little. Secure the flower to the stem. Finish the rest of the flowers as the top ones and attach to the small i-cords. Sew in the ends of the flowers by turning them inside out.

Pin and sew the small stems to the main stem, sewing on both sides of the i-cord. Insert florist's wire into the main stem, up to a little way down from the top flower to let this droop down. Secure the cast-on edge of the i-cord.

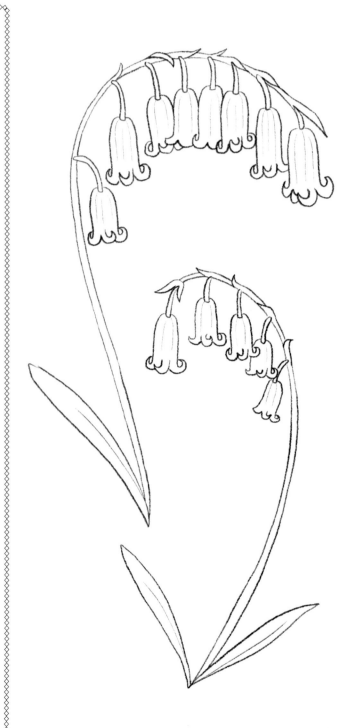

Bluebell

15

Carnation *Dianthus caryophyllus*

Carnation petals have a delicate look with ruffled edges, and a spicy clove-like scent. The flowers are traditionally pink but there are varieties in red, pink, yellow, white and even green! They symbolize love, distinction and motherly affection.

Materials

Small amounts of 4-ply yarn in pale pink (A) and cerise (B)

Small amount of DK yarn in light green (C)

Pair each of 3.25mm (UK10:US3) and 3.75mm (UK9:US5) knitting needles or a circular needle

Pair of 3.75mm (UK9:US5) double-pointed knitting needles

Tapestry needle

Florist's wire

Small amount of cotton wool

Finished size

10in (25cm) long
Flower: 7cm (2¾in) wide

Tip

The flower starts as a large number of stitches, then decreases to create the ruffles.

Pattern

Flower

Using B and 3.25mm needles, cast on 200 sts.

Change to A, leaving a length of yarn.

St st 6 rows, starting with a k row.

Row 7: (K2tog) to end (100 sts).

Row 8: (P2tog) to end (50 sts).

Row 9: (K2tog) to end (25 sts).

Row 10: (P2tog) to last st, p1 (13 sts).

Row 11: (K2tog) to last st, k1 (7 sts).

Row 12: P.

Cast off rem sts.

Stem and cup

Using C and 3.75mm dpns, cast on 3 sts, leaving a length of yarn.

Make an i-cord 8in (20cm) long.

Transfer to 3.75mm straight needles, ready for a p row.

Row 1: P.

Row 2: K1, m1, k1, m1, k1 (5 sts).

Row 3: P.

Row 4: K1, m1, k1, m1, k2, m1, k1 (8 sts).

Row 5: P.

Row 6: K1, m1, k3, m1, k3, m1, k1 (11 sts).

Row 7: P.

Row 8: K1, m1, k4, m1, k5, m1, k1 (14 sts).

St st 5 rows.

Next row (RS): P.

Cast off, leaving a length of yarn.

To make up

Sew in the ends on the cast-on edge. Sew the side seam. With the length of yarn from the cast-off edge, wrap the yarn a few times around the bottom of the flower to close up the ruffles a little, and secure, leaving a length of yarn. Take the length of yarn at the bottom of the flower and thread through the top of the stem.

Sew the seam of the cup, stuffing lightly with cotton wool as you sew. Secure the flower into the cup, catching the flower but not going through to the front of the cup. Insert the florist wire into the stem and secure the cast-on edge.

Cherry Blossom *Prunus serrulata*

Cherry blossom, also known as Japanese cherry, is the national flower of Japan. The delicate pink or white flowers grow in clusters on the tree branches and are only in bloom for a short time. The flowers symbolize renewal, growth and a new beginning.

Materials

Small amount of 4-ply yarn in light pink (A) and cerise (B)

Small amount of DK yarn in dark brown (C)

Pair of 3.25mm (UK10:US3) knitting needles

Pair of 3.75mm (UK9:US5) double-pointed knitting needles

Tapestry needle

Florist's wire

Finished size

7in (18cm) long
Flowers: 1in (2.5cm) wide

Tip

The twigs are i-cords stiffened with florist's wire so that they keep their shape.

Pattern

Flowers (make 8)
Using A and 3.25mm needles, cast on 24 sts,
leaving a length of yarn.
Row 1: P.
Row 2: (K2tog) to end (12 sts).
Row 3: (P2tog) to end (6 sts).
Row 4: (K2tog) to end (3 sts).
Cast off rem sts.

Twigs
Main twig
Using C and 3.75mm dpns, cast on 3 sts,
leaving a length of yarn.
Make an i-cord 7in (18cm) long.
Cast off.
Small twigs (make 2)
Using C and 3.75mm dpns, cast on 3 sts.
Make an i-cord 2in (5cm) long.
Cast off.

To make up
Flowers
Sew the seam, starting at the cast-off edge. Thread the yarn
through the cast on edge, gather and secure. Push the centre
of the flower to the WS. On the WS, using the length of yarn,
wrap around the bottom of the flower a few times, a little up
from the centre, to create a less even shape, taking the yarn
out of the centre on the WS. Using B, embroider French
knots (see page 139) onto the centre of each flower.

Twigs
Insert a length of florist's wire through the main piece and
secure the ends. Sew in the cast-on end. Do the same with
the shorter twigs. Attach the flowers to the twigs, sewing
two flowers to the ends of the twigs. Attach the smaller twigs
to the main twig, sewing all around the twig and a little way
up the sides. Thread the yarn down through the twigs. Use
C to sew around the base of the flowers to cover where they
have been sewn on to the twigs in A.

Cherry Blossom

Clematis *Clematis*

Part of the buttercup family, this climbing plant has large delicate flowers, often in purples and pinks, some with stripes on the petals. The flowers symbolize wisdom, mental acuity, aspiration and travel.

Materials

Small amounts of DK yarn in pink (A), cerise (B), yellow (C) and cream (D)

Pair of 3.75mm (UK9:US5) knitting needles

Tapestry needle

Finished size

4½in (11.5cm) wide

Tip

The flower is made up of two sections, with two lots of three petals, worked individually. Chain-stitch embroidery forms the stripes on the petals.

Pattern

Flowers (make 2 pieces)
Using A, cast on 9 sts.
K one row.
Work on the first 3 sts as folls:
Row 1: P.
Row 2: K1, m1, k1, m1, k1 (5 sts).
Row 3: K1, p3, k1.
Row 4: K1, m1, k3, m1, k1 (7 sts).
Row 5: K1, p5, k1.
Row 6: K1, m1, k to last st, m1, k1 (9 sts).
St st 9 rows, keeping k1 at the beginning and
end of the WS rows.
Row 16: K2tog, k to last 2 sts, k2tog (7 sts).
Row 17: K1, p to last st, k1.
Row 18: K2tog, k3, k2tog (5 sts).
Row 19: K1, p3, k1.
Row 20: K2tog, k1, k2tog (3 sts).
Row 21: Sl 1, p2tog, psso.
Fasten off rem st.
Cut the yarn and attach to the next st.
Rep until 3 petals have been made.

Centre
Using C, cast on 15 sts.
K 1 row.
Cast off p wise, leaving a length of yarn.

To make up
Sew in the ends of the petals, leaving a length of yarn
at the cast-on edge. Block and press the pieces.

On each of the groups of three, sew the ends of the petals
together. Thread the yarn through the cast-on edges,
gather and secure, sewing a little way up the sides of the
petals. Using B and chain stitch (see page 139), embroider
lines on the petals, using the photo as a guide. Place one
piece on top of the other and sew in place. Sew a little way
up the sides of the petals to secure one set to the other.

Roll the centre, then use the length of yarn to secure in
place, taking the yarn through to the opposite side a few
times. Using D, start at the back of the centre and make
four loops at the front, securing each at the back.
Sew this finished tab onto the flower.

Cornflower *Anemone coronaria*

With its striking colour and feathery petals, cornflowers symbolize, among other things, a positive hope for the future. It used to grow as a weed in cornfields, which is where its name derives from, and it is also known as 'bachelor's button'.

Materials

Small amount of 4-ply yarn in blue (A)

Small amount of DK yarn in dark green (B)

Pair each of 3.25mm (UK10:US3) and 3.75mm (UK9:US5) knitting needles

Pair of 3.75mm (UK9:US5) double-pointed knitting needles

Tapestry needle

Pins

Finished size

7½in (19cm) long
Flower: 1½in (4cm) wide

Tip

The petals are two sections sewn together, each knitted in one piece working on a few stitches at a time, with a picot cast-off edge.

Pattern

Flowers (make 2)

Using A and 3.25mm needles, cast on 9 sts.
Starting with a RS row, st st 6 rows.
Work on the first 3 sts as folls:
Row 1: K.
Row 2: P.
Row 3: K1, m1, k1, m1, k1 (5 sts).
Row 4: P.
Row 5: K1, m1, k3, m1, k1 (7 sts).
Row 6: P.
Row 7: K1, m1, k to last st, m1, k1 (9 sts).
Row 8: P.
Row 9: (picot cast-off):
Cast off 2 sts, * sl rem st on right-hand needle onto
left-hand needle, cast on 2 sts, cast off 4 sts; rep from
* to end, fasten off the remaining st, leaving a length
of yarn.
Cut the yarn and attach it to the next st.
Rep rows 1–9 until 3 petals have been made.

Cup and stem

Using B and 3.75mm needles, cast on 12 sts,
leaving a length of yarn.
Row 1: K.
Row 2: K.
Row 3: P.
Row 4: K.
Row 5: P2tog, p3, p2tog, p3, p2tog (9 sts).
Row 6: K2tog, k2, k2tog, k1, k2tog (6 sts).
Row 7: P2tog, p2, p2tog (4 sts).
Row 8: K2tog, k2 (3 sts).
St st 2 rows.
Transfer sts to 3.75mm dpns.
Make an i-cord 6in (15cm) long.
Cast off, leaving a length of yarn.

Leaves (make 2)

Using B and 3.75mm needles, cast on 3 sts,
leaving a length of yarn.

St st 12 rows, starting with a k row.
Row 13: Sl 1, k2tog, psso.
Fasten off rem st.

To make up

Sew in the ends of the flower, leaving a length of yarn at
the cast-on edge. Pin the two pieces of the flower together,
with the WS facing. Sew the bottom seam and the side
seams up to the picot cast-off. Sew the rest of the sides
of the flower, leaving the cast-off edges open.

Sew the side seam of the cup. Fold the base of the flower
in half, and place inside the cup at the top of the i-cord.
Thread the yarn through the top of the cup, gather and
secure. Secure the flower inside the cup and sew around
the top of the cup. Sew the leaves onto the stem, sewing
a little way up the sides of the leaves.

Crocus *Crocus sativus*

The crocus, native to woodland and a familiar sight in spring, is part of the iris family. The dried stigmas have been used since ancient times to produce saffron, one of the world's most expensive spices. This has been knitted in purple, but crocus flowers can be yellow, orange or white too.

Materials

Small amounts of DK yarn in purple (A), dark green (B) and yellow (C)

Pair of 3.75 (UK9:US5) knitting needles

Pair of 3.25mm (UK10:US3) double-pointed knitting needles

Tapestry needle

Finished size

6¾in (17cm) long
Flower: 1½in (4cm) wide

Tip

The flower is knitted in one piece, working on each petal individually. The stem and stamens are i-cords and the leaves are worked separately.

Pattern

Flower

Using A and 3.75mm needles, cast on 18 sts, leaving a length of yarn.

K one row.

Work on the first 3 sts as folls:

Row 1: K.

Row 2: P.

Row 3: K1, m1, k1, m1, k1 (5 sts).

St st 9 rows.

Row 13: K2tog, k1, k2tog (3 sts).

Row 14: P.

Row 15: Sl 1, k2tog, psso.

Fasten off rem st, cut yarn and attach to the next st.

Rep rows 1 to 15 until 6 petals have been made.

Stem

Using B and 3.25mm dpns, cast on 4 sts.

Work an i-cord to 5in (13cm).

Transfer sts to 3.75mm needles.

Next row: P.

Row 1: K1, m1, k2, m1, k1 (6 sts).

Row 2: P.

Row 3: K1, m1, k to last st, m1, k1 (8 sts).

Row 4: P.

Row 5: K1, m1, k to last st, m1, k1 (10 sts).

Row 6: P.

Row 7: K1, m1, k to last st, m1, k1 (12 sts).

Row 8: P1, m1p, p5, m1p, p5, m1p, p1 (15 sts).

Cast off, leaving a length of yarn.

Leaves (make 2)

Using B and 3.75mm needles, cast on 3 sts, leaving a length of yarn.

Row 1: P.

Row 2: K1, m1, k1, m1, k1 (5 sts).

St st 7 rows.

Row 10: K2tog, k1, k2tog (3 sts).

St st 9 rows.

Row 20: Sl 1, k2tog, psso.

Fasten off rem st.

Stamen

Using C and 3.75mm needles, cast on 7 sts.

Cast off k wise, leaving a length of yarn.

To make up

Sew in the ends of the flower, leaving a length of yarn at one end of the cast-on edge. Sew the first to the last petal. Thread the yarn through the cast-on edge, gather and secure with the RS facing outwards. Wrap the yarn a few times around the bottom of the flower to pull the petals together and secure.

Sew the side seam of the cup. Pull the stamen inside the flower using the length of yarn, turn the flower inside out and secure to the bottom of the flower. Leave the length of yarn on the stamen. Turn the cup at the top of the stem inside out and sew the bottom of the flower to the centre of the cup. Turn the right way out. Thread the yarn through the cast-off edge of the cup and pull to gather slightly. Secure and neaten the end.

Sew the cast-off edges of the leaves. Block and press. Using the length of yarn at the cast-on edge, sew onto the bottom of the stem on both sides and a little way up the sides of the leaves.

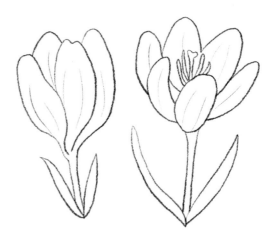

Daffodil *Narcissus*

Daffodils are one of the first spring flowers to bloom, bringing colour to the landscape with their cheerful yellow. The familiar flowers have a central trumpet surrounded by six petal-like sepals and are often seen in meadows and woods.

Materials

Small amounts of DK yarn in yellow (A) and orange (B)

Pair of 3.75mm (UK9:US5) knitting needles

Tapestry needle

Pins

Small piece of yellow felt

Finished size

4in (10cm) wide

Tip

The outer petals are knitted in one piece with each petal worked individually. The trumpet or corona is knitted as a rectangle with a picot cast-off edge gathered at the bottom.

Pattern

Petals

Using A, cast on 35 sts, leaving a length of yarn.
K 2 rows.
Working on the first 7 sts, work as folls:
Row 1: K.
Row 2: K1, p to last st, k1.
Row 3: K.
Row 4: K1, p to last st, k1.
Row 5: K.
Row 6: K1, p to last st, K1.
Row 7: K2tog, k to last 2 sts, k2tog (5 sts).
Row 8: K1, p3, k1.
Row 9: K2tog, k1, k2tog (3 sts).
Row 10: K1, p1, k1.
Row 11: Sl 1, k2tog, psso.
Fasten off rem st.
Cut the yarn and attach to the next st.
Rep rows 1–11 until 5 petals have been worked.

Centre

Using A, cast on 17 sts, leaving a length of yarn.
K 6 rows.
Picot cast-off
Cast off 2 sts, * sl rem st on right-hand needle onto left-hand needle, cast on 2 sts, cast off 4 sts; rep from * to end, fasten off the remaining st.

To make up
Sew the side seam of the centre piece. Thread the yarn through the cast-on edge, gather and secure.

Block and press the main piece. Sew the main piece cast-on and cast-off ends together, joining a little way up between the petals. Thread the yarn through the cast-on edge and gather, leaving a hole at the centre so that the petals lie flat. Place the centre onto the main piece and secure. Neaten the back of the flower.

Stamens (make 3)

Using B, cut a length of yarn approx 4in (10cm) long, fold it in half and place a pin at the halfway point. Pin into a soft surface. Tie knots in the two strands of yarn until it measures 1in (2.5cm) long. Using the lengths of yarn at the end of the knots, thread through the centre of the back of the flower. Tie the yarn a few times and trim the ends.

Cut out a small circle of yellow felt and sew it to the back of the flower to neaten.

Daisy *Bellis perennis*

Sometimes called lawn daisy or English daisy, these are a familiar sight in garden lawns. The name daisy is thought to originate from the Old English 'day's eye', because the petals close at night and open in the morning; the term 'fresh as a daisy' implies that someone is refreshed after a good rest!

Materials

Small amounts of DK yarn in cream (A) and yellow (B)

Pair of 3.75mm (UK9:US5) knitting needles

Tapestry needle

Finished size

3½in (9cm) wide

Tip

This simple flower is made up of two pieces. The petals are worked in garter stitch in one piece, with a few stitches being worked for each petal. The centre is shaped in garter stitch, and gathered to form a bobble.

Pattern

Petals

Using A, cast on 15 sts,
leaving a length of yarn.
K one row.
*** Row 1:** working on the first 3 sts, k3.
Row 2: K1, m1, k1, m1, k1 (5 sts).
Row 3: K.
Row 4: K1, m1, k to last st, m1, k1 (7 sts).
K 10 rows.
Row 15: K2tog, k3, k2tog (5 sts).
Row 16: K.
Row 17: K2tog, k1, k2tog (3 sts).
Row 18: Sl 1, k2tog, psso.
Fasten off remaining st. *
Cut the yarn and attach it to the next st.
Repeat from * to * until 5 petals have
been made.

Centre

Using B, cast on 3 sts.
Row 1: K.
Row 2: K1, m1, k1, m1, k1 (5 sts).
Row 3: K1, m1, k to last st, m1, k1 (7 sts).
K 5 rows.
Row 9: K2tog, k3, k2tog (5 sts).
Row 10: K2tog, k1, k2tog (3 sts).
Cast off rem sts, leaving a length of yarn.

To make up

Sew in the ends, leaving a length of yarn on the
cast-on edge of the main piece and on one end
of the centre piece. Join the first and last petal.
Thread the yarn through the cast-on edge and
gather. Thread the yarn around the centre
piece and gather to form a bobble. Attach
this to the centre of the main piece.

Daisy

Forget-me-not *Myosotis*

Clouds of these delicate, small blue flowers appear in flower borders, verges and woodlands during spring. They traditionally symbolize remembrance, with other meanings including devotion and true love.

Materials

Small amounts of 4-ply yarn in light blue (A), dark green (B) and yellow (C)

Pair of 3.25mm (UK10:US3) knitting needles

Pair of 3.25mm (UK10:US3) double-pointed knitting needles

Tapestry needle

Ribbon, ¼in (6mm) wide x 17¾in (45cm) long

Finished size

5¾in (14.5cm) long
Flowers: 1¼in (3.5cm) wide

Tip

The petals are knitted in one piece with an embroidered French knot at the centre; the stems are i-cords.

Pattern

Flowers (make 4)
Using A and 3.25mm needles,
cast on 15 sts, leaving a length of yarn.
Work on the first 3 sts as folls:
Row 1: P.
Row 2: K1, m1, k1, m1, k1 (5 sts).
Row 3: P.
Row 4: K2tog, k1, k2tog (3 sts).
Row 5: Sl 1, p2tog, psso.
Fasten off rem st.
Cut the yarn and attach to the next st.
Rep rows 1–5 until 5 petals have
been made.

Stems (make 4)
Using B and 3.25mm dpns,
cast on 3 sts, leaving a length of yarn.
Make an i-cord 5½in (14cm) long.
Cast off, leaving a length of yarn.

To make up
Sew in the ends on the petals, leaving
the length of yarn at the cast-on edge.
Block and press. Sew the first to the
last petal, leaving a length of yarn.
Thread the yarn through the cast-off
edge, gather and secure. Using C,
embroider a French knot (see page 139)
at the centre of each flower, leaving the
ends of the yarn at the back. Using A,
sew the flowers onto the top of the stems.
Use B to sew over where the flowers
have been attached. Thread the yarn at
the back of the French knots through
the top of the i-cord a little way down
and cut. Cut the ends of the ribbon in
a V shape to neaten. Wrap around the
stems and tie in a bow.

Foxglove *Digitalis purpurea*

These striking flowers, most commonly pink, purple and white, are tubular and trumpet-like in shape around a tall stem. Foxgloves are considered to be wildflowers, and the scientific name digitalis derives from the Latin for 'finger-like'.

Materials

Small amounts of DK yarn in light purple (A) and light green (B)

Pair of 3.75mm (UK9:US5) knitting needles

Pair of 3.75mm (UK9:US5) double-pointed knitting needles

Tapestry needle

Florist's wire or a wooden skewer

Finished size

9½in (24cm) long

Tip

Open and closed flowers are worked individually and sit inside cups. The stem is an i-cord; the leaves are worked separately.

Pattern

Open flowers (make 6)

Using A and 3.75mm needles, cast on 13 sts, leaving a length of yarn.

Row 1: K.
Row 2: K.
Row 3: P.
Row 4: K.
Row 5: P.
Row 6: K2tog, k3, k2tog, k4, k2tog (10 sts).
Row 7: P2tog, p2, p2tog, p2, p2tog (7 sts).
Row 8: K2tog, k1, k2tog, k2tog (4 sts).
Cast off rem sts, leaving a length of yarn.

Closed flowers (make 3)

Using A and 3.75mm needles, cast on 9 sts, leaving a length of yarn.

Row 1: K.
Row 2: P.
Row 3: K2tog, k1, k2tog, k2, k2tog (6 sts).
Row 4: (P2tog) to end (3 sts).
Row 5: Sl 1, k2tog, psso.
Fasten off rem st, leaving a length of yarn.

Cup for open flowers (make 6)

Using B and 3.75mm needles, cast on 11 sts, leaving a length of yarn.

Row 1: K.
Row 2: K.
Row 3: P.
Row 4: K.
Row 5: P2tog, p2, p2tog, p3, p2tog (8 sts).

Row 6: K2tog, k1, k2tog, k1, k2tog (5 sts).
Row 7: P2tog, p1, p2tog (3 sts).
Row 8: K.
Row 9: Sl 1, p2tog, psso.
Fasten off rem st, leaving a length of yarn.

Cup for closed flowers (make 3)

Using B and 3.75mm needles, cast on 9 sts.

Row 1: K.
Row 2: K.
Row 3: P2tog, p1, p2tog, p2, p2tog (6 sts).
Row 4: (K2tog) to end (3 sts).
Row 5: P.
Row 6: Sl 1, k2tog, psso.
Fasten off rem st.

Stem

Using B and 3.75mm dpns, cast on 4 sts, leaving a length of yarn. Make an i-cord 8½in (22cm) long. Cast off, leaving a length of yarn.

Leaves (make 2)

Using B and 3.75mm needles, cast on 3 sts, leaving a length of yarn.

Row 1: P.
Row 2: K1, m1, k1, m1, k1 (5 sts).
St st 17 rows.
Row 20: K2tog, k1, k2tog (3 sts).
Row 21: Sl 1, p2tog, psso.
Fasten off rem st, leaving a length of yarn.

Shorter leaves (make 2)

Make as for the longer leaves, working 13 rows st st instead of 17 rows.

To make up

Sew in the cast-on ends of the flowers and cups. Sew the seams of the flowers and cups, leaving a length of yarn at the cast-off edges. Thread the yarn through the top of the closed flowers, gather and secure. Place the flowers inside the cups and sew in place by threading the yarn from the flower through the centre of the cup. Sew along the top of the cup in B to hold the flower in place. Sew in the yarn for the flower. Leave a length of yarn on the bottom of the cups.

Sew one of the closed flowers to the top of the stem so that it is facing upwards, by sewing a little way up the side of the cup. Insert a length of florist's wire or a wooden kebab stick through the stem and secure the cast-on end. Sew the other two closed flowers near the top of the stem. Sew the open flowers onto the stem further down. Sew the leaves onto the stem, placing the longer leaves below the shorter ones. Sew a little way up the sides of the leaves to make them point upwards.

Fuchsia *Fuchsia*

Native to America and New Zealand, fuchsias have pendulous flowers normally consisting of two colours. The flower has associations with being cheerful, playful and uplifting, the name originating from the colour.

Materials

Small amounts of 4-ply yarn in cerise (A), purple (B), dark green (C)

Pair of 3.25mm (UK10:US3) knitting needles

Pair of 3.25mm (UK10:US3) double-pointed knitting needles

Stitch holder

Tapestry needle

Finished size

7in (18cm) long
Flower: 3½in (9cm) wide

Tip

The outer petals are worked individually and put onto a stitch holder, and the inner is knitted in one piece, working on a group of stitches at a time. The stem is an i-cord and the stamens are knotted yarn.

Pattern

Outer petals

Using A and 3.25mm needles, cast on 3 sts, leaving a length of yarn.

Row 1: P.
Row 2: K1, m1, k1, m1, k1 (5 sts).
Row 3: P.
Row 4: K1, m1, k3, m1, k1 (7 sts).
Rows 5–12: St st.

Put these sts on a holder.

Make 3 more petals, working rows 1–12, add the sts for the first 2 to the holder, then add the 3 on the holder back to the needle along with the fourth petal (28 sts).

St st 4 rows, starting with a p row.

Next row: (P2tog) to end (14 sts).
Next row: (K2tog) to end (7 sts).
Next row: P2tog, p3, p2tog (5 sts).

Change to C, and put these 5 sts onto 3.25mm dpns.

Work an i-cord to 5½in (14cm).

Cast off.

Inner petals

Using B and 3.25mm needles, cast on 15 sts, leaving a length of yarn.

St st 6 rows, starting with a RS row.

Work on the first 5 sts as folls:

Row 7 (RS): K.
Row 8: P.
Row 9: K.
Row 10: P2tog, p1, p2tog (3 sts).
Row 11: Sl 1, k2tog, psso.

Cut the yarn, leaving a length, attach it to the next st.

Rep rows 7–11 until 3 petals have been made.

Stamens (make 3)

Using A, cut a length of yarn approx 6in (16cm) long, fold it in half and place a pin at the halfway point. Pin into a soft surface. Tie knots in the two strands of yarn until it measures 1½in (4cm) long.

Using the lengths of yarn at the end of the knots, thread through the centre of the back of the flower. Tie the yarn a few times and trim the ends.

Make one more stamen as above using 7in (18cm) yarn and tying knots until it measures about 2¼in (6cm) long.

To make up

Sew in the ends on the petals, leaving a length of yarn at the cast-on edges. Block and press the petals. Sew the first and last petals of the inner piece together to halfway up the petals.

Thread the yarn through the cast-off edge, gather and secure, leaving a length of yarn. Place this piece into the centre of the main flower and secure to the top of the stem with the length of yarn, sewing the end into the top of the stem to neaten.

Using the length of yarn on the main flower, join the first to the last petal and sew a little way up so that the seam is the same depth as the rest of the petals. Using the ends of the yarn on the stamens, thread through the centre of the inner section, and bring the ends through the bottom of the main flower. Thread the ends through the sides of the main flower on the WS and cut.

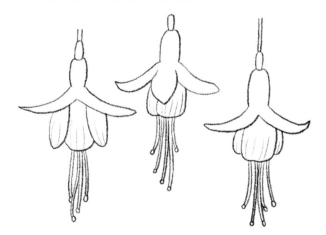

Gerbera *Gerbera*

Native to South Africa, gerberas have a wide range of bright colours and a tufted, daisy-like appearance. There's bound to be a gerbera out there to match most colours in your stash, so make them in whatever shades you like.

Materials

Small amounts of DK yarn in cerise (A), red (B) and brown (C)

Pair of 3.75mm (UK9:US5) knitting needles

Tapestry needle

Finished size

4in (10cm) wide

Tip

The petals are made in one piece by casting off and on stitches. Two layers form the main part of the flower. The centre is a rolled tab with a shaped bobble in the middle.

Pattern

Main piece (make 2)
Using A, cast on 12 sts.
Row 1: P.
Row 2: K.
Row 3: Cast off 9 sts pwise, p2 (3 sts).
Row 4: K3, turn, cast on 9 sts (12 sts).
Rep rows 1-4 until 10 petals have been worked,
ending on a row 3.
Cast off rem sts.

Tab
Using B, cast on 15 sts, leaving a length of yarn.
Cast off.

Centre
Using C, cast on 3 sts, leaving a length of yarn.
Row 1: K.
Row 2: K1, m1, k1, m1, k1 (5 sts).
K 3 rows.
Row 6: K2tog, k1, k2tog (3 sts).
Row 7: Sl 1, k2tog, psso.
Fasten off rem st.

To make up
Sew the first to the last petal on the main pieces.
Sew in the ends, leaving a length of yarn on the
cast-on edge of the main pieces. Thread the yarn
through the cast-on edge of each piece, gather
and secure. Sew the two pieces together with RS
facing upwards.

Roll the tab from the end without the length of
yarn, and sew the end in place, then sew through
the rolled tab a few times to secure. Thread the
yarn around the edge of the centre and gather
to form a bobble. Sew the bobble onto the rolled
tab, then sew the rolled tab onto the centre
of the flower.

Hyacinth *Hyacinthus*

Native to the eastern Mediterranean, hyacinths are bold, colourful and fragrant spring-flowering plants grown from bulbs, with small, dense flowers around a thick stem. Originally a pale violet or blue colour, hyacinths now come in a large range of shades including white, cream, pink, yellow, purple and orange.

Materials

Small amount of 4-ply yarn in light blue (A)

Small amounts of DK yarn in dark green (B), beige (C) and light brown (D)

Pair of 3.75mm (UK9:US5) knitting needles

Pair of 3.25mm (UK10:US3) knitting needles

Pins

Tapestry needle

Piece of dark brown felt

Toy stuffing

Piece of card

Finished size

Container: 3in (8cm)
wide x 2½in (6cm) deep
Total height: 6¾in (17cm)

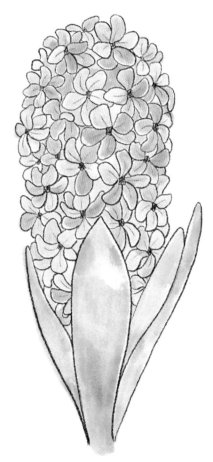

Tip

The small flowers are knitted by casting off and on stitches.

Pattern

Flowers (make 20)
Using A and 3.25mm needles,
cast on 5 sts, leaving a length of yarn.
Row 1: P.
Row 2: K.
Row 3: Cast off 3 sts p wise,
p to end (2 sts).
Row 4: K2, turn, cast on 3 sts (5 sts).
Rep rows 1–4 three times more, ending
on a row 3, and leaving a length of yarn.

Stem
Using B and 3.75mm needles,
cast on 16 sts, leaving a length of yarn.
St st to 3½in (9cm), ending on a WS row.
Row 1 (dec): K2tog, k3, k2tog, k3,
k2tog, k2, k2tog (12 sts).
Row 2: P2tog, p3, p2tog, p3,
p2tog (9 sts).
Row 3: (K2tog) to last st, k1 (5 sts).
Cast off.

Leaves (make 2)
Using B and 3.75mm needles,
cast on 3 sts, leaving a length of yarn.
Row 1: P.
Row 2: K1, m1, k1, m1, k1 (5 sts).
Row 3 and every alt row: K1,
p to last st, k1.
Row 4: K1, m1, k to last st, m1, k1
(7 sts).
St st 9 rows.
Row 14: K2tog, k to last 2 sts, k2tog
(5 sts).
Row 15: K1, p to last st, k1.
Row 16: K2tog, k1, k2tog (3 sts).
Row 17: P.
Row 18: Sl 1, k2tog, psso.
Fasten off rem st.

Bulb
Using D and 3.75mm needles,
cast on 5 sts.
Row 1: P.
Row 2: K1, (m1, k1) to end (9 sts).
Row 3 and every alt row: P.
Row 4: K1, (m1, k1) to end (17 sts).
Row 6: K1, (m1, k2) to end (25 sts).
Row 8: K1, (m1, k3) to end (33 sts).
St st 5 rows.
Next row (RS): P.
Cast off, leaving a length of yarn.

Container
Using C and 3.75mm needles,
cast on 5 sts.
Row 1: P.
Row 2: K1, (m1, k1) to end (9 sts).
Row 3 and every alt row: P.
Row 4: K1, (m1, k1) to end (17 sts).
Row 6: K1, (m1, k2) to end (25 sts).
Row 8: K1, (m1, k3) to end (33 sts).
Row 10: K1, (m1, k4) to end (41 sts).
Row 12: K1, (m1, k5) to end (49 sts).
Row 13: P.
Side
Next row: (K1, p1) to end.
Rep this row until side measures
4in (10cm).
Cast off.

To make up
Flowers
Sew the first to the last petal,
leaving a length of yarn.

Stem
Sew the side seam, stuffing
with toy stuffing as you sew.

Bulb
Sew the side seam. Stuff with toy
stuffing. Pin the bulb around the
bottom of the stem and sew in place.
Pin the flowers onto the stem and
sew in place, leaving the bottom of
the stem without flowers to attach
the leaves.

Leaves
Sew in the cast-off ends. Block and
press. Sew the leaves onto the base
of the stem just above the bulb, and
a little way up the sides of the leaves.

Container
Sew the side seam from the centre
outwards to 1in (2.5cm) below the top.
Sew up the rest of the seam from the
inside. Turn over the top 1in (2.5cm)
and sew a few times along the cast-off
edge to secure. Cut a circle of card to
fit the base of the pot and place inside.
Stuff the container with toy stuffing.

Earth
Cut out a circle of felt to fit the top
of the container. Cut a smaller circle
at the centre to place the bottom part
of the bulb in. Place the felt circle
into the container, and pin around
the sides. Sew around the edge of
the felt to secure the circle to the
sides of the container.

Hyacinth

63

Lavender *Lavandula angustifolia*

Lavender's distinctive appearance and scent make it a popular garden plant. Essential oils are extracted from the flowers, which are also used as dried flowers, both for their pleasant and relaxing scent. The flowers symbolize purity, serenity, grace and calmness.

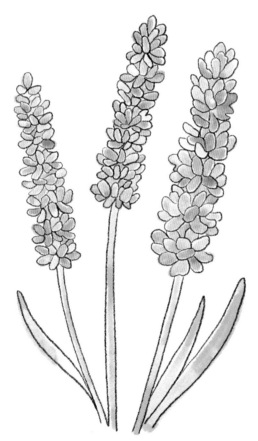

Materials

Small amounts of DK yarn in lilac (A) and light green (B)

Pair of 3.75mm (UK9:US5) knitting needles

Pair of 3.75mm (UK9:US5) double-pointed knitting needles

Ribbon, ⅜in (1cm) wide x 17½in (45cm) long

Tapestry needle

Finished size

6in (15cm) long
Flowers: 2¼in (6cm) long x ¾in (2cm) wide

Tip

The flowers are worked in a mini bobble stitch. The stems are i-cords and the flowers wrap around these.

Abbreviation

MB: make bobble: work (p1, k1, p1, k1) all in next st, pass 2nd, 3rd and 4th sts over first st.

Pattern

Flowers (make 3)
Using A and 3.75mm needles,
cast on 9 sts, leaving a length of yarn.
Row 1 (RS): K.
Row 2: K1, *MB, k1;
rep from * to end.
Row 3: K.
Row 4: K2, *MB, k1;
rep from * to last st, k1.
Rep these 4 rows until work
measures 2½in (6cm) from
cast-on edge, or to the
length of flowers preferred.
Cast off.

Stem (make 3)
Using B and 3.75mm dpns,
cast on 4 sts.
Work an i-cord to
4¾in (12cm).

To make up
Sew in the ends of the stems. Pin the
flower section around the stem, with
the stem starting a little way down
from the top of the flower. Sew in
place, sewing the seam and securing
the bottom of the flowers to the stem.
Gather the top of the flower section
and secure.

Cut a length of ribbon and cut the
ends in a V shape. Tie around the
stems in a bow.

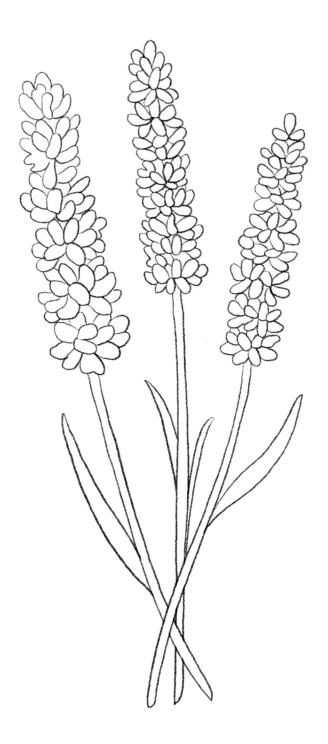

Lilac *Syringa vulgaris*

Lilac is a species of woody plants in the olive family, native to woodland and scrubland. The pale purple colour is the most recognizable, but lilac can also be white, pink, yellow or burgundy. The purple flowers symbolize spirituality, the white purity and innocence.

Materials

Small amounts of DK yarn in light mauve (A), lilac (B), damson (C) and dark green (D)

Pair of 3.75mm (UK9:US5) knitting needles

Pair of 3.75mm (UK9:US5) double-pointed needles

Tapestry needle

Pins

Toy stuffing

Florist's wire

Finished size

7¾in (20cm) long
Flower: 4¾in (12cm) long

Tip

The flower is knitted in a textured bobble pattern, using three colours, to mimic the real-life flowers found on the bloom.

Pattern

Stitch pattern (uneven number of sts)
Row 1: K1 A, * work 1 flake in B as folls: work (k1, yo, pass k st over yo and return rem st to left-hand needle) 3 times, leaving last yo st on right-hand needle, k1 A; rep from * to end.
Row 2: Using A, p.
Row 3: Using C, work 1 flake as before, *k1 A, work 1 flake in C; rep from * to end.
Row 4: Using A, p.
Rep these 4 rows.

Flower
Using C, cast on 10 sts, leaving a length of yarn.
St st 2 rows, starting with a k row.
Inc and work the stitch pattern as folls:
Row 1: K1, m1, work patt to last st, m1, k1 (12 sts).
Row 2: P1, m1p, work patt to last st, m1p, p1 (14 sts).
Row 3: K1, m1, patt to last st, m1, k1 (16 sts).
Row 4: P1, m1p, patt to last st, m1p, p1 (18 sts).
Row 5: K1, m1, patt to last st, m1, k1 (20 sts).
Work without shaping for 2 rows.
Dec.
Row 8: K2tog, patt to last 2 sts, k2tog (18 sts).
Row 9 and every alt row: P.
Row 10: K2tog, patt to last 2 sts, k2tog (16 sts).
Row 12: K2tog, patt to last 2 sts, k2tog (14 sts).
Row 14: K2tog, patt to last 2 sts, k2tog (12 sts).
Row 16: K2tog, patt to last 2 sts, k2tog (10 sts).
Row 18: K2tog, patt to last 2 sts, k2tog (8 sts).
Row 20: K2tog, patt to last 2 sts, k2tog (6 sts).
Using C, st st 2 rows.
Cast off rem sts.

Leaves (make 2)
Using D and 3.75mm needles, cast on 3 sts.
Row 1: P.
Row 2: K1, m1, k1, m1, k1 (5 sts).
Row 3: K1, p to last st, k1.
Row 4: K1, m1, k to last st, m1, k1 (7 sts).

Row 5: K1, p to last st, k1.
Row 6: K1, m1, k to last st, m1, k1 (9 sts).
St st 11 rows, keeping k1 at the end of each p row.
Row 18: K2tog, k to last 2 sts, k2tog (7 sts).
Row 19: K1, p to last st, k1.
Row 20: K2tog, k3, k2tog (5 sts).
Row 21: K1, p3, k1.
Row 22: K2tog, k1, k2tog (3 sts).
Row 23: K1, p1, k1.
Row 24: Sl 1, k2tog, psso.
Fasten off rem st.

Stem
Using D and 3.75 dpns, cast on 4 sts, leaving a length of yarn.
Work an i-cord to 4¾in (12cm).
Cast off.

To make up
Sew in the ends of the main piece and the cast-off edges of the leaves. Block and press the leaves.

Pin the seam of the flower and sew up using C, starting at the cast-off edge and sewing close to the first flakes, stuffing lightly as you sew. Leave an opening at the cast-on edge.

Attach the leaves to the stem, and sew a little way up the sides of the leaf. Use the yarn at the top of the i-cord to thread through the base of the flower, push the i-cord a little way in and secure the base of the flower to the stem. Insert the wire into the stem and push up into the flower. Secure the cast-on edge of the stem.

Lily *Lilium*

Lilies are grown from bulbs, with large, often fragrant prominent flowers. They come in a wide range of colours, and some have markings such as spots or stripes.

Materials

Small amounts of DK yarn in pink (A), purple (B), cerise (C) and green (D)

Pair of 3.75mm (UK9:US5)

knitting needles

Tapestry needle

Finished size

5in (13cm) wide

Tip

Chain stitch and straight stitch embroidery are used for the markings on the petals.

Pattern

Petals (make 2 pieces)
Using A, cast on 9 sts.
Work on first 3 sts as folls:
Row 1: P.
Row 2: K1, m1, k1, m1, k1 (5 sts).
Row 3 and every alt row: K1, p to last st, k1.
Row 4: K1, m1, k to last st, m1, k1 (7 sts).
Row 6: K1, m1, k to last st, m1, k1 (9 sts).
Row 8: K1, m1, k to last st, m1, k1 (11 sts).
St st 9 rows, keeping k1 at the beginning
and end of the p rows.
Row 18: K2tog, k to last 2 sts, k2tog (9 sts).
Row 19 and every alt row: K1, p to last st, k1.
Row 20: K2tog, k to last 2 sts, k2tog (7 sts).
Row 22: K2tog, k3, k2tog (5 sts).
Row 24: K2tog, k1, k2tog (3 sts).
Row 26: Sl 1, k2tog, psso.
Fasten off rem st.
Cut yarn and attach to the next st.
Rep rows 1–26 until 3 petals have been made.

Centre (rolled tab)
Using A, cast on 15 sts.
K 1 row.
Cast off.

Stamens (make 3)
Using D, cut 3 x 3in (8cm) strands of yarn for each stamen.
Plait to 1½in (3.5cm), starting and ending with a knot.

To make up
Sew in the ends of the cast-off ends of the petals.
Block and press the petals. Using yarn C, embroider
chain stitch (see page 139) at the centre of the petals.
Using yarn B, embroider small dashes in straight stitch
(see page 139) around the centre line.

Roll the centre tab and secure, threading the yarn through
to the other side of the tab a few times. Sew the stamens
onto the centre of the tab, leaving one of the knotted ends
at the back. Sew the rolled tab onto the centre of the flower.

Lily

Pansy *Viola tricolor*

Pansies are popular bedding plants with large colourful flowers and distinctively shaped petals with clear markings. The name is thought to originate from the French word *pensée*, meaning 'thought'. It symbolizes friendship, and a gift of pansies shows that you are thinking of someone.

Materials

Small amounts of DK yarn
in cream (A), purple (B),
dark green (C) and yellow (D)

Pair of 3.75mm (UK9:US5)
knitting needles

Tapestry needle

Finished size

6¼in (16cm) wide including leaves
Flower: 4in (10cm) wide

Tip

The front petals are worked in intarsia
and the back petals and leaves in one
colour. The centre is shaped and
gathered to form a bobble.

Pattern

Note: the front petals are knitted in intarsia, divide yarn A into two balls before starting.

Front petals (make 3)
Using A, cast on 3 sts, leaving length of yarn.
P one row.
Row 1: K1, m1, k1, m1, k1 (5 sts).
Row 2: K1, p3, k1.
Row 3: K1, m1, k to last st, m1, k1 (7 sts).
Row 4: K1A, p1A, p3B, p1A, k1 A.
Row 5: K1A, m1, k1A, k3B, k1A, m1, k1A. (9 sts).
Row 6: K1A, p1A, p5B, p1A, k1A.
Row 7: K1A, m1, k1A, k5B, k1A, m1, k1A (11 sts).
Row 8: K1A, p2A, p5B, p2A, k1A.
Row 9: K1A, m1, k3A, k3B, k3A, m1, k1A (13 sts).
Row 10: K1A, p4A, p3B, p4A, k1A.
With A only, st st 2 rows.
Row 13: K2tog, k to last 2 sts, k2tog (11 sts).
Row 14: K2tog, p to last 2 sts, k2tog (9 sts).
Row 15: K2tog, k to last 2 sts, k2tog (7 sts).
Row 16: K2tog, p to last 2 sts, k2tog (5 sts).
Row 17: K2tog, k1, k2tog (3 sts).
Row 18: Sl 1, p2tog, psso.

Back petals (make 2)
Using B only, work as for front petals without the intarsia, adding 2 extra st st rows between rows 10 and 13 (20 rows in total).

Leaves (make 3)
Using C, cast on 3 sts, leaving length of yarn.
Row 1: P.
Row 2: K1, m1, k1, m1, k1 (5 sts).
Row 3 and every alt row: K1, p to last st, k1.
Row 4: K1, m1, k to last st, m1, k1 (7 sts).
Row 6: K1, m1, k to last st, m1, k1 (9 sts).
Row 8: K1, m1, k to last st, m1, k1 (11 sts).
Row 10: K1, m1, k to last st, m1, k1 (13 sts).
St st 9 rows.

Row 18: K2tog, k to last st, k2tog (11 sts).
Row 20: K2tog, k to last st, k2tog (9 sts).
Row 22: K2tog, k to last st, k2tog (7 sts).
Row 24: K2tog, k to last st, k2tog (5 sts).
Row 26: K2tog, k to last st, k2tog (3 sts).
Row 27: Sl 1, p2tog, psso.
Fasten off rem st.

Centre (make 3)
Using D, cast on 3 sts, leaving a length of yarn.
Row 1: P.
Row 2: K1, m1, k1, m1, k1 (5 sts).
St st 3 rows.
Row 6: K2tog, k1, k2tog (3 sts).
Row 7: Sl 1, p2tog, psso.
Fasten off rem st.

To make up
Sew in the cast-off ends of the petals and leaves.
Sew in the ends on the intarsia sections.
Block and press the petals and leaves.

Sew the leaves together at the centre, at the cast-on edges, and a little way up the sides to keep them in place. Do the same with the front petals. Sew the back petals to the front petals, slightly to the side. Use the length of yarn on the back petals to catch onto the purple part of the front petals from the back so that it doesn't show on the front.

Thread the yarn around the edge of the centre and gather to form a bobble. Secure. Sew the bobble onto the centre of the petals. Sew the petals onto the leaves from the back using yarn C, not going through to the front of the flowers.

Pansy

79

Passion Flower *Passiflora*

Passion flowers are climbing plants with dramatic flowers, often bluish with purple and feathery filaments. The flowers symbolize purity, strength and calm.

Materials

Small amounts of 4-ply yarn in white (A), purple (B) and yellow (C)

Pair of 3.25mm (UK10:US3) knitting needles

Tapestry needle

Finished size

4in (10cm) wide

Tip

The flower is made up of five sections. The petals are worked individually and sit on a circular base. The fringe base is a rolled tab, and the stamens are worked by casting off and on stitches.

Pattern

Petals (make 8)
Using A, cast on 3 sts, leaving a length of yarn.
Row 1: K.
Row 2: P.
Row 3: K1, m1, k1, m1, k1 (5 sts).
St st 14 rows
Row 18: P2tog, p1, p2tog (3 sts).
Row 19: K.
Row 20: Sl 1, p2tog, psso.
Fasten off rem st.

Base
Using A, cast on 5 sts, leaving a length of yarn.
Row 1: P.
Row 2: K1, (m1, k1) to end (9 sts).
Row 3 and every alt row: P.
Row 4: K1, (m1, k1) to end (17 sts).
Row 6: K1, (m1, k2) to end (25 sts).
Row 8: K1, (m1, k3) to end (33 sts).
Row 10: K1, (m1, k4) to end (41 sts).
Row 11: P.
Row 12: K.
Cast off.

Fringe base
Using A, cast on 40 sts, leaving a length of yarn.
K 2 rows.
Cast off.

Stamens
Using C, cast on 8 sts, leaving a length of yarn.
Row 1: P.
Row 2: K.
Row 3: Cast off 5 sts, p to end (3 sts)
Row 4: K3, turn, cast on 5 sts (8 sts).
Rep rows 1–4 until 4 sections have been worked,
ending on a row 3.
Cast off.

Inner stamens
Using B, work as for the stamens, until 3 sections
have been worked.

To make up
Sew in the cast-off ends of the petals. Block and press.
Sew the seam of the base circle. Block and press. With
RS facing upwards, pin four of the petals onto the base
opposite each other with the cast-on edges at the centre.
Sew in place up to the edge of the circle. Pin the other
four petals between these and sew in place up to the
edge of the circle.

Roll the tab for the tassel base up and secure, taking
the yarn through to the opposite side a few times;
leave a length of yarn. Cut 2 lengths of yarn for each
tassel, 2½in (10cm) long. Form a tassel and thread
through the edges of the rolled tab base. Trim to
¾in (2cm) long.

Sew the first to the last sections on the stamens and
inner stamens. Thread the yarn through the cast-on
edges of each, gather with the RS facing outwards,
and secure. Leave the stamens piece slightly open.
Place the inner stamens inside the stamens and sew
in place through to the back. Secure the stamens
at the gathered edge.

Thread the yarn from the bottom of the two pieces
through the centre of the rolled tab fringe base
and secure. Sew the rolled tab tassel base onto
the centre of the flower.

Peace Lily *Spathiphyllum*

This evergreen plant has a distinctive sheath or spade-like white protective leaf called a spathe, with a spike of flowers inside. It symbolizes peace, purity and healing.

Materials

Small amounts of DK yarn in white (A), dark green (B) and yellow (C)

Pair of 3.75mm (UK9:US5) knitting needles

Pair of 3.25mm (UK10:US3) double-pointed knitting needles

Tapestry needle

Finished size

7½in (19cm) long
Flower: 3in (7.5cm) long
x 2¼in (6cm) wide (unfurled)

Tip

The stem starts as an i-cord with the stitches transferred to straight needles. The main part is worked with increases and decreases, and the flower spike is a small i-cord.

Pattern

Stem
Using B and dpns, cast on 4 sts.
Make an i-cord 4¾in (12cm) long.
Transfer to 3.75mm needles, ready for a p row.
Next row: P.
Next row: K1, (kfb in next st) to end (7 sts).
Next row: P.
Next row: K1, (kfb, k1) to end (10 sts).
Change to A.

Flower
Row 1 and every WS row: K1, p to last st, k1.
Row 2: K1, kfb, k3, kfb, k2, kfb, k1 (13 sts).
Row 4: K1, kfb, k3, kfb, k3, kfb, k3 (16 sts).
Row 6: K.
Row 8: K1, kfb, k5, kfb, k5, kfb, k2 (19 sts).
Row 10: K1, kfb, k6, kfb, k6, kfb, k3 (22 sts).
St st 3 rows.
Row 14 (dec): K2tog, k8, k2tog, k to last 2 sts, k2tog (19 sts).
Row 15: K1, p to last st, k1.
Row 16: K2tog, k7, k2tog, k to last 2 sts, k2tog (16 sts).
Row 17: P2tog, p5, p2tog, p to last 2 sts, p2tog (13 sts).
Row 18: K2tog, k4, k2tog, k to last 2 sts, k2tog (10 sts).
Row 19: P2tog, p2, p2tog, p2, p2tog (7 sts).
Row 20: K2tog, k3, k2tog (5 sts).
Row 21: P2tog, p1, p2tog (3 sts).
Row 22: Sl 1, k2tog, psso.
Fasten off rem st.

Stamen
Using C and dpns, cast on 3 sts, leaving a length of yarn.
Work an i-cord to 2in (5cm).
Cast off.

To make up
Sew in the cast-on end of the flower, threading the yarn
down the edge of the flower to neaten. Do not press.

Sew in the cast-off edge of the stamen. Place the stamen
into the top of the stem and pull the length of yarn at the
cast-on edge down through the stem. Secure with B
at the top of the stem.

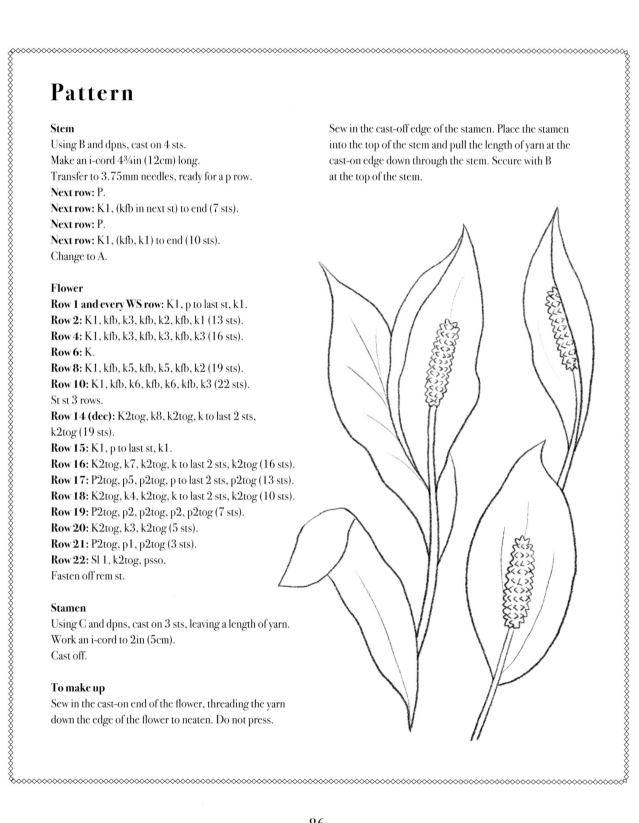

Poinsettia *Euphorbia pulcherrima*

Native to Mexico and Central America, poinsettia's paper-like red petals and dark green leaves are often associated with Christmas, and it is the birth flower for December. The flower symbolizes success and good cheer.

Materials

Small amounts of DK yarn in red (A), dark green (B) and ochre (C)

Pair of 3.75mm (UK9:US5) knitting needles

Pair of 3.75mm (UK9:US5) double-pointed knitting needles

Beads

Tapestry needle

Sewing needle and thread

Finished size

4in (10cm) wide

Tip

The flower is made up of five petals worked separately, and three leaves. The centre is a rolled i-cord with beads in the middle.

Pattern

Petals (make 5)
Using A and 3.75mm needles, cast on 3 sts, leaving a length of yarn.
Row 1: P.
Row 2: K1, m1, k1, m1, k1 (5 sts).
Row 3 and every alt row: K1, p to last st, k1.
Row 4: K1, m1, k3, m1, k1 (7 sts).
Row 6: K1, m1, k to last st, m1, k1 (9 sts).
St st 7 rows, keeping k1 at each end of WS rows.
Row 14: K2tog, k to last 2 sts, k2tog (7 sts).
Row 16: K2tog, k3, k2tog (5 sts).
Row 18: K2tog, k1, k2tog (3 sts).
Row 19: Sl 1, p2tog, psso.
Fasten off rem st.

Leaves (make 3)
Using B and 3.75mm needles, cast on 3 sts, leaving a length of yarn.
Row 1: P.
Row 2: K1, m1, k1, m1, k1 (5 sts).
Row 3 and every alt row: K1, p to last st, k1.
Row 4: K1, m1, k3, m1, k1 (7 sts).
Row 6: K1, m1, k to last st, m1, k1 (9 sts).
St st 9 rows, keeping k1 at each end of WS rows.
Row 16: K2tog, k to last 2 sts, k2tog (7 sts).
Row 18: K2tog, k3, k2tog (5 sts).
Row 20: K2tog, k1, k2tog (3 sts).
Row 21: Sl 1, p2tog, psso.
Fasten off rem st.

Centre
Using C and 3.75mm dpns, cast on 4 sts.
Make an i-cord 2½in (6cm) long.
Cast off.

To make up
Sew in the cast-off ends of the petals and leaves.
Block and press.

Pin the five petals together at the cast-on edges. Sew them together, sewing a little way up the back to join the petals.

Pin the three leaves together at the cast-on edge and sew together as for the petals.

Roll the i-cord tab, and secure, taking the yarn through to the opposite side a few times. Sew the beads onto the rolled centre. Sew the centre onto the flower. Sew the flower onto the leaves.

Poppy *Papaver rhoeas*

With their large, delicate petals and distinctive centres, red poppies are a familiar sight along roadside verges. Different colours are associated with peace and remembrance, so you could make your poppy in white, purple or black, if you prefer.

Materials

Small amounts of DK yarn in red (A), purple (B) and black (C)

Pair of 3.75mm (UK9:US5) knitting needles

Tapestry needle

Finished size

3½in (9cm) wide

Tip

The flower is made up of four individual petals, sewn together at the centre. The centre is a rolled tab with a group of embroidered French knots in the middle.

Pattern

Petals (make 4)
Using A, cast on 3 sts, leaving a length of yarn.
Row 1: P.
Row 2: K1, m1, k1, m1, k1 (5 sts).
Row 3 and every WS row: K1, p to last st, k1.
Row 4: K1, m1, k3, m1, k1 (7 sts).
Row 6: K1, m1, k5, m1, k1 (9 sts).
Row 8: K1, m1, k7, m1, k1 (11 sts).
Row 10: K1, m1, k to last st, m1, k1 (13 sts).
St st 3 rows, keeping k1 at the beginning
and end of the WS rows.
Row 14: K2tog, k to last 2 sts, k2tog (11 sts).
Row 15: K2tog, p to last 2 sts, k2tog (9 sts).
Row 16: K2tog, k to last 2 sts, k2tog (7 sts).
Row 17: K2tog, p to last 2 sts, k2tog (5 sts).
Cast off rem sts.

Centre
Tab
Using B, cast on 15 sts, leaving a length of yarn.
K one row.
Cast off.

To make up
Sew in the cast-off ends of the petals, leaving the
length of yarn at the cast-on edges. Block and press.
Sew two petals together at the cast-on edges and
a little way up the sides. Repeat for the other two.
Place one pair of petals on top of the other and
sew in place.

Roll the tab, starting at the end without the length
of yarn, and sew in place, taking the yarn through
the rolled tab to the other side a few times to secure.
Using C, embroider a group of French knots
(see page 139) at the centre of the rolled tab.
Sew the rolled tab onto the centre of the petals.

Primrose *Primula vulgaris*

Primroses derive their name from the Latin *primus*, meaning first, as they are one of the first flowers to bloom in spring. They are commonly found in woodlands and hedgerows, and symbolize renewal, youth and optimism.

Materials

Small amount of 4-ply yarn in pale yellow (A) and yellow (C)

Small amount of DK yarn in dark green (B)

Pair of 3.25mm (UK10:US3) knitting needles

Pair of 3.75mm (UK9:US5) knitting needles

Tapestry needle

Finished size

4in (10cm) wide

Tip

The flowers are made as a rectangle with a row of eyelets in the middle; these are then folded and gathered. The leaves are worked separately; the flowers are sewn onto these.

Pattern

Flowers (make 3)
Using A and 3.25mm needles, cast on 16 sts, leaving a length of yarn.
St st 5 rows, starting with a WS row.
Row 6 (RS): K1, (k2tog, yo, k1) to end.
St st 5 rows.
Cast off, leaving a length of yarn.

Leaves (make 3)
Using B and 3.75mm needles, cast on 3 sts, leaving a length of yarn.
Row 1: P
Row 2: K1, m1, k1, m1, k1 (5 sts).
Row 3: K1, p3, k1.
Row 4: K1, m1, k3, m1, k1 (7 sts).
Row 5: K1, p5, k1.
Row 6: K1, m1, k to last st, m1, k1 (9 sts).
St st 9 rows, keeping k1 at the beginning and end of the p rows.
Row 15: K2tog, k to last 2 sts, k2tog (7 sts).
Row 16: K1, p to last st, k1.
Row 17: K2tog, k3, k2tog (5 sts).
Row 18: K1, p3, k1.
Row 19: K2tog, k1, k2tog (3 sts).
Row 20: Sl 1, p2tog, psso.
Fasten off rem st.

To make up
Sew in the cast-off ends of the leaves.
Block and press the leaves.

Fold the flower along the eyelet line. Sew the side seams using the length of yarn at the cast-on and cast-off edges. Thread the yarn through each of the cast-on and cast-off sides and gather. Secure at the centre. Flatten so that the eyelets are around the outside, and secure at the centre. Leave the length of yarn to sew onto the leaves. Using C, embroider French knots (see page 139) at the flower centres.

With a length of yarn, sew the cast-on edges of the leaves together, sewing a little way up where the leaves join to secure. Pin the flowers to the centre of the leaves, and sew from the back using B, catching the yarn through the flowers but not through to the top.

Primrose

99

Rose *Rosa*

The ever-popular rose has over 300 species, including climbing varieties, and is known for its distinctive layered and fragranced flowers. Different colours have different symbolism: red for romantic love, white for innocence, yellow for friendship and pink for gratitude and admiration.

Materials

Small amount of 4-ply yarn in pink (A)

Small amount of DK yarn in dark green (B)

Pair of 3.25mm (UK10:US3) knitting needles

Pair of 3.75mm (UK9:US5) double-pointed knitting needles

Florist's wire

Tapestry needle

Finished size

9¾in (28cm) long
Flower: 1½in (4cm) wide
x 2¼in (6cm) high

Tip

The flower is made up of six outer petals and four inner petals, worked individually and wrapped to form the shape.

Pattern

Outer petals (make 6)
Using A and 3.25mm needles,
cast on 3 sts.
Row 1 and every alt row: P.
Row 2: K1, m1, k1, m1, k1 (5 sts).
Row 4: K1, m1, k3, m1, k1 (7 sts).
Row 6: K1, m1, k to last st, m1, k1
(9 sts).
Row 8: K1, m1, k to last st, m1, k1
(11 sts).
St st 5 rows.
Row 14: K2tog, k7, k2tog (9 sts).
Row 15: P.
Row 16: K2tog, k5, k2tog (7 sts).
Row 17: P2tog, p3, p2tog (5 sts).
Row 18: K2tog, k1, k2tog (3 sts).
Row 19: Sl 1, p2tog, psso.
Fasten off rem st.

Inner petals (make 4)
Work as for outer petals from row
1 to row 8.
St st 9 rows.
Work as for outer petals from row
14 to end.

Stem
Using B and 3.75 dpns, cast on 3 sts.
Work an i-cord to 8¾in (22cm).
Transfer to 3.75mm needles,
ready to start with a p row.
Row 1: P.
Row 2: K1, m1, k1, m1, k1 (5 sts).
Row 3: P1, m1p, p3, m1p, p1 (7 sts).
Row 4: K1, m1, k2, m1, k3, m1, k1
(10 sts).
Row 5: P1, m1p, p4, m1p, p4, m1p,
p1 (13 sts).

Row 6: K1, m1, k5, m1, k6, m1, k1
(16 sts).
Row 7: P.
Work on the first 4 sts as folls:
Row 8: K.
Row 9: P.
Row 10: K.
Row 11: (P2tog) to end (2 sts).
Row 12: K2tog.
Fasten off rem st.
Cut the yarn aand attach it to the next st.
Rep rows 8–12 three times more.

Stem with leaf
Using B and 3.75mm dpns, cast on 3 sts.
Work an i-cord to 1¼in (3cm).
Transfer to 3.75mm needles,
ready for a p row.
Row 1: P.
Row 2: K1, m1, k2 (4 sts).
Work on the first 2 sts as folls:
Row 3: P.
Row 4: K1, m1, k1 (3 sts).
Row 5: P1, m1, p1, m1, p1 (5 sts).
Row 6: K.
Row 7: P.
Row 8: K2tog, k1, k2tog (3 sts).
Row 9: Sl 1, p2tog, psso.
Fasten off rem st.
Cut the yarn and attach it to the next st.
Work on rem 2 sts, rep rows 3–9.

To make up
Sew in the ends on the cast-off edges
of the petals and leaf. Block and press
the petals.

Pin the inner 4 petals together in a
line overlapping slightly. Sew together,
both on the outside and inside. Roll
up the piece and secure the edge of
the last stitch to one of the other petals.
Sew up the outer petals in the same
way as the inner petals in a line. Wrap
these around the inner petals and sew
in place. The inner petals should be
longer than the outer petals. Thread
the yarn through the cast-on edges of
the petals and pull to gather. Secure
the outer petals through to the inside
of the inner petals a few times. Sew
the first to the last piece at the top
of the main stem, sewing a little way
up the seam.

Pin the stem to the bottom of the
flower, spread the leaves out and sew
in place. Insert the florist's wire into
the main stem and secure the cast-on
edge. Do the same with the small stem.
Sew the small stem to the main stem,
sewing a little way up the sides of the
stem to keep it in place.

Snowdrop *Galanthus*

One of the first flowers to bloom after winter, snowdrops symbolize rebirth, new beginnings and hope. The name describes their delicate bell-shaped white flowers that resemble a drop of snow, and they can often grow in snow.

Materials

Small amounts of 4-ply yarn in white (A) and dark green (B)

Pair of 3.25mm (UK10:US3) needles

Pair of 3.75mm (UK9:US5) double-pointed knitting needles

Tapestry needle

Finished size

7in (18cm) long
Flower and cup: 1¾in (4.5cm) long

Tip

The main flower is knitted in one piece with each of the four petals worked individually. The stem is an i-cord with the stitches transferred to straight needles to knit the cup. The leaves are worked separately.

Pattern

Flower

With A and 3.25mm needles, cast on 12 sts.

K 2 rows.

Work on the first 3 sts as folls:

Row 1: K.

Row 2: P.

Row 3: K1, m1, k1, m1, k1 (5 sts).

St st 8 rows.

Row 12: P2tog, p1, p2tog (3 sts).

Row 13: Sl 1, k2tog, psso.

Fasten off rem st.

Cut the yarn and attach it to the next st.

Rep rows 1–13 until 4 petals have been worked.

Stem

Using B and 3.25mm dpns, cast on 5 sts.

Work an i-cord to 5½in (14cm).

Transfer to 3.25mm needles.

Row 1 (WS): P.

Row 2: K1, m1, k3, m1, k1 (7 sts).

Row 3: P.

Row 4: K1, m1, k5, m1, k1 (9 sts).

Row 5: P.

Row 6: K1, m1, k3, m1, k4, m1, k1 (12 sts).

Row 7: P.

Row 8: K1, m1, k5, m1, k5, m1, k1 (15 sts).

Cast off.

Leaf (make 2)

Using B and 3.25mm needles, cast on 3 sts.

Row 1: P.

Row 2: K1, m1, k1, m1, k1 (5 sts).

St st 20 rows.

Row 23: P2tog, p1, p2tog (3 sts).

Row 24: Sl 1, k2tog, psso.

Fasten off rem st.

To make up

(do not press the petals)

Sew in the ends of the petals, leaving a length of yarn on the cast-on edge. Sew the first to the last petal, thread the yarn through the cast-on edge, gather and secure.

Sew in the cast-off ends of the leaves. Block and press.

Sew the seam of the cup at the top of the stem. Place the flower inside the cup, with RS outwards, and sew in place.

Sew the leaves onto the stem.

Sunflower *Helianthus*

Sunflowers, part of the daisy family, are distinctive for their tall stems and dramatic large flowers. The name derives from the Greek name for the sun (*helios*), as they resemble the sun and typically bloom in summer. They are associated with cheerfulness and happiness.

Materials

Small amounts of DK yarn in yellow (A), ochre (B), brown (C), dark brown (D) and black (E)

Pair of 3.75mm (UK9:US5) knitting needles

Tapestry needle

Finished size

4½in (11.5cm) wide

Tip

The centre is knitted flat in a circle made by increasing stitches. The petals are knitted in one piece, with each petal being worked individually. Embroidered French knots add texture to the centre section.

Pattern

Petals

Using B, cast on 49 sts, leaving a length of yarn.

K 2 rows.

Change to A.

Work on the first 7 sts as folls:

Row 1 (RS): K.

Row 2: K1, p5, k1.

Rep these 2 rows once more.

Row 5: K2tog, k3, k2tog (5 sts).

Row 6: P2tog, p1, p2tog (3 sts).

Row 7: K2tog, k1 (2 sts).

Row 8: P2tog.

Cut the yarn and attach to the next st.

Rep rows 1–8 until 7 petals have been worked.

Centre

Using C, cast on 5 sts, leaving a length of yarn.

Row 1: P.

Row 2: K1, (m1, k1) to end.

Row 3 and every alt row: P.

Row 4: K1, (m1, k1) to end (17 sts).

Row 6: K1, (m1, k2) to end (25 sts).

Row 8: K1, (m1, k3) to end (33 sts).

Row 10: K1, (m1, k4) to end (41 sts).

Row 11: P.

Cast off.

To make up

Sew in the ends of the petals, leaving a length of yarn
at the cast-on edge. Sew the side seam of the centre
piece. Block and press these pieces.

Sew the first to the last petal. Pin the petals around
the edge of the centre piece and sew in place using B.
Embroider French knots (see page 139) around the
edge of the centre piece with B, around the centre
in C and at the centre in E.

Thistle *Cirsium vulgare*

Part of the daisy family, thistles have a series of sharp points around a cup shape that holds the flower. The rounded head of the flower is made up of small feather-like petals. The thistle symbolizes protection, deriving from its prickly leaves, and it is the national flower of Scotland.

Materials

Small amounts of DK yarn in mauve (A) and light green (B)

Pair of 3.75mm (UK9:US5) knitting needles

Pair of 3.75mm (UK9:US5) double-pointed knitting needles

Florist's wire

Tapestry needle

Finished size

7in (18cm)
Flower and cup: 2½in (6cm) long

Tip

The stem is worked from the top by decreasing to form the cup, with the stitches then transferred to dpns for an i-cord stem.

113

Pattern

Outer petals

Using A and 3.75mm needles, cast on 12 sts, leaving a length of yarn.

Row 1: Cast off 11 sts (1 st), turn.
Row 2: Cast on 11 sts (12 sts).
Rep rows 1 and 2 until 8 petals made.

Inner petals

Using A and 3.75mm needles, cast on 9 sts, leaving a length of yarn.

Row 1: Cast off 8 sts (1 st), turn.
Row 2: Cast on 8 sts (9 sts).
Rep rows 1 and 2 until 6 petals made.

Cup and stem

Using B and 3.75mm needles, cast on 16 sts, leaving a length of yarn.

Row 1 (RS): P.
Row 2: (K1, p1) to end (moss st).
Row 3: (P1, k1) to end.
Row 4: As row 2.
Row 5: As row 3.
Row 6: As row 2.
Row 7: P2tog, moss st 6, p2tog, moss st 4, k2tog (13 sts).
Row 8: P2tog, moss st 4, k2tog, moss st 3, k2tog (10 sts).
Row 9: P2tog, moss st 2, p2tog, moss st 2, k2tog (7 sts).
Row 10: P2tog, k1, p2tog, k2tog (4 sts).
Row 11: P.
Transfer to 3.75mm dpns.
Work an i-cord to 5½in (14cm).
Cast off.

Leaves (make 2)

Using B and 3.75mm needles, cast on 8 sts, leaving a length of yarn.

Row 1: K.
Row 2: K.
Row 3: Picot cast-off as folls:

Cast off 2 sts, * sl rem st on right-hand needle onto left-hand needle, cast on 2 sts, cast off 4 sts; rep from * to end, fasten off the remaining st, leaving a length of yarn.

To make up

Sew the seam on the cup, leaving a length of yarn. Sew the leaves onto the stem opposite each other, sewing from both sides.

Sew the first to the last petal on the inner and outer petals. Thread the yarn through the cast-on edge, gather and secure. With RS facing outwards, place the two pieces of the flower inside the cup. Turn the cup inside out and secure the flower to the centre by catching the edges of the flower but not going through to the outside. Turn the cup the right way out. Thread the yarn through the top of the cup and pull slightly to gather. Secure around the flower.

Insert a length of florist's wire through the stem and a little way inside the cup and secure the cast-on end.

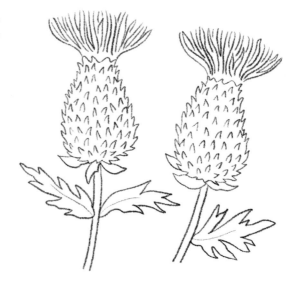

Thistle

Tulip *Tulipa*

These cheerful spring-flowering plants have large, brightly coloured petals. The national flower of both Turkey and Iran, the name tulip comes from the Persian word for turban, *delband*.

Materials

Small amounts of DK yarn in orange (A), dark green (B) and yellow (C)

Pair of 3.75mm (UK9:US5) knitting needles

Pair of 3.75mm (UK9:US5) double-pointed knitting needles

Tapestry needle

Toy stuffing or cotton wool, small amount

Wooden skewer or florist's wire

Finished size

9¾in (25cm) long

Tip

The four petals are worked individually, and wrap around a stuffed inner piece. The stem is an i-cord, and the leaf is worked separately.

Pattern

Petals (make 4)
Using A and 3.75mm needles, cast on 3 sts, leaving a length of yarn.
Row 1 and every alt row: P.
Row 2: K1, m1, k1, m1, k1 (5 sts).
Row 4: K1, m1, k3, m1, k1 (7 sts).
Row 6: K1, m1, k to last st, m1, k1 (9 sts).
Row 8: K1, m1, k to last st, m1, k1 (11 sts).
St st 4 rows.
Row 13: P2tog, p7, p2tog (9 sts).
Row 14: K2tog, k5, k2tog (7 sts).
Row 15: P2tog, p3 p2tog (5 sts).
Row 16: K2tog, k1, k2tog (3 sts).
Row 17: Sl 1, p2tog, psso.
Fasten off rem st.

Inner
Using A and 3.75mm needles, cast on 5 sts, leaving a length of yarn.
Row 1: P.
Row 2: K1, inc in next st, k1, inc in next st, k1, inc in next st, k1, inc in next st, k1 (9 sts).
Row 3: P.
Row 4: K1, (m1, k1) to end (17 sts).
Row 5: P.
Row 6: K1 (m1, k2) to end (25 sts).
St st 3 rows.
Row 10: (K2tog) to last st, k1 (13 sts).
Row 11: P2tog to last st, p1 (7 sts).
Row 12: K2tog to last st, k1 (4 sts).
Row 13: (Ktog) to end (2 sts).
Cast off rem sts.

Stem
Using B and 3.75mm dpns, cast on 4 sts, leaving a length of yarn.
Make an i-cord 8in (20cm) long.
Cast off, leaving a length of yarn.

Leaf
Using B and 3.75mm needles, cast on 3 sts.
Row 1: K.
Row 2: P.
Row 3: K1, m1, k1, m1, k1 (5 sts).
St st 17 rows.
Row 21: K2tog, k1, k2tog (3 sts).
Row 22: Sl 1, p2tog, psso.
Fasten off rem st.

Stamens (make 3)
Using C, cut 3 x 4in (10cm) lengths of yarn, and knot at the top. Make a plait to ¾in (2cm), finishing with a knot.

To make up
Sew in the cast-off ends of the petals and leaf.
Block and press the petals and leaf.

Sew the seam on the inner piece, starting at the top and stuffing it as you sew, leaving an opening at the bottom for the stem. Place a kebab stick or florist's wire into the stem. Secure the ends.

Put the top end of the stem inside the opening in the inner and secure. Pin two of the petals to the inner, opposite each other and sew in place. Pin the other two petals to the inner and sew in place. They will overlap slightly.

Sew the leaf to the stem, sewing a little way up the sides.

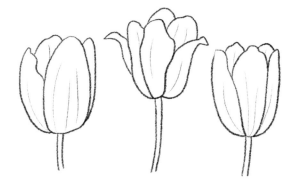

African Violet *Saintpaulia ionantha*

With its small, vividly coloured flowers and velvety leaves, this compact houseplant flowers in early spring. The flowers symbolize modesty and humility, and a pot of African violets is a traditional February birthday gift.

Materials

Small amounts of 4-ply yarn in purple (A) and pale yellow (D)

Small amounts of DK yarn in dark green (B)

Small amount of Aran yarn in stone (C)

Pair of 3.25mm (UK10:US3) knitting needles

Pair of 3.75mm (UK9:US5) knitting needles

Pair of 4.5mm (UK7:US7) knitting needles

Tapestry needle

Toy stuffing

Piece of card

Finished size

Pot: 2¼in (5.5cm) wide, 1½in (4cm) high
Flowers and leaves: 3¾in (9.5cm) wide

Tip

The flowers are made in one piece, with the petals worked individually. The leaves are knitted separately, and the container starts with a circular base with a basket-stitch side.

Pattern

Flowers (make 5)
Using A and 3.25mm needles,
cast on 15 sts, leaving a length of yarn.
P one row.
Work on the first 3 sts as folls:
Row 1: K.
Row 2: P.
Row 3: K1, m1, k1, m1, k1 (5 sts).
Row 4: P.
Row 5: K.
Row 6: P2tog, p1, p2tog (3 sts).
Row 7: Sl 1, k2tog, psso.
Fasten off rem st.
Cut the yarn and join it to the next st.
Rep rows 1–7 until 5 petals have been
worked.

Leaves (make 5)
Using B and 3.75mm needles,
cast on 3 sts, leaving a length of yarn.
Row 1: P.
Row 2: K1, m1, k1, m1, k1 (5 sts).
Row 3: P1, m1p, p3, m1p, p1 (7 sts)
Row 4: K1, m1, k to last st, m1, k1
(9 sts).
Row 5: P1, m1p, p to last st, m1p, p1
(11 sts).
St st 8 rows.
Row 14: K2tog, k to last 2 sts, k2tog
(9 sts).
Row 15: P2tog, p to last 2 sts, p2tog
(7 sts).
Row 16: K2tog, k3, k2tog (5 sts).
Row 17: P2tog, p1, p2tog (3 sts).
Row 18: Sl 1, k2tog, psso.
Fasten off rem st.

Container
Using C and 4.5mm needles,
cast on 5 sts.
Row 1: P.
Row 2: K1, (m1, k1) to end (9 sts).
Row 3 and every alt row: P.
Row 4: K1, (m1, k1) to end (17 sts).
Row 6: K1, (m1, k2) to end (25 sts).
Row 8: K1, (m1, k3) to end (33 sts).
Row 9 (WS): K to mark turn,
inc 2 sts over two of the increases
made previously (35 sts).
Side
Row 1 and every alt row: K.
Row 2: *K3, p1; rep from * to last
3 sts, k3.
Row 4: As row 2.
Row 6: K1, *p1, k3; rep from * to
last 2 sts, p1, k1.
Row 8: As row 6.
Rep these 8 rows until 13 rows have
been worked.
Next row (WS): K.
Next row (RS): P.
Cast off.

To make up
Sew in the ends of the petals. Join the
cast-on and cast-off edges. Thread the yarn
through the cast-on edge from the RS and
gather, leaving a length of yarn. Using D,
embroider three French knots (see page
139) at the centre of the flowers.

Sew the base and side seams of the
container. Cut a card circle to fit the
base of the container and put inside.

Sew in the cast-off ends of the
leaves. Block and press. Pin the
leaves together at the cast-on edges
in a circle, slightly overlapping each
other. Sew together, sewing a little
way up the side of each leaf.

Pin the flowers onto the leaves, and
sew in place, first three then two
on top of these. Thread the ends of
the flowers and the French knots
through to the back.

Put toy stuffing into the container.
Using C, sew around the top of the
container, catching the underside
of the leaves without going through
to the top.

Water Lily *Nymphaea*

Water lilies are rooted in soil at the bottom of ponds, with the flowers and leaves sitting on the surface. The leaves are large and plate-like, and the flowers, most commonly pink or white, have layers of petals.

Materials

Small amounts of DK yarn in pink (A) and ochre (B)

Pair of 3.75mm (UK9:US5) knitting needles

Tapestry needle

Pins

Finished size

5in (13cm) wide

Tip

Inner and outer petals are knitted in one piece, working on each petal individually. The inner piece is worked by casting off and on stitches, and the flower sits on a circular base.

Pattern

Outer petals
Using A, cast on 32 sts,
leaving a length of yarn.
K 2 rows.
Work on the first 4 sts as folls:
Row 1: P.
Row 2: K1, m1, k2, m1, k1 (6 sts).
Row 3: K1, p to last st, k1.
Row 4: K1, m1, k4, m1, k1 (8 sts).
St st 7 rows, keeping k1 at the
beginning and end of the p rows.
Row 12: K2tog, k4, k2tog (6 sts).
Row 13: K1, p to last st, k1.
Row 14: K2tog, k2, k2tog (4 sts).
Row 15: K1, p2, k1.
Row 16: (K2tog) to end (2 sts).
Row 17: P2tog.
Fasten off rem st.
Cut the yarn and attach to the next st.
Rep from row 1 to row 17 until
8 petals have been worked.

Middle petals
Using A, cast on 18 sts,
leaving a length of yarn.
K 2 rows.
Work on the first 3 sts as folls:
Row 1: P.
Row 2: K1, m1, k1, m1, k1 (5 sts).
Row 3: K1, p3, k1.
Row 4: K3, m1, k2 (6 sts).
St st 7 rows, keeping k1 at each end
of WS rows.
Row 12: K2tog, k2, k2tog (4 sts).
Row 13: K1, p2, k1.
Row 14: (K2tog) to end (2 sts).
Row 15: P2tog.
Fasten off rem st.

Cut the yarn and attach to the next st.
Rep rows 1–15 until 6 petals have
been worked.

Inner
Using B, cast on 8 sts,
leaving a length of yarn.
Row 1: P.
Row 2: K.
Row 3: Cast off 5 sts, p2 (3 sts).
Row 4: K3, turn, cast on 5 sts (8 sts).
Rep rows 1–4 until 6 sections have
been worked, ending on a row 3.
Cast off rem sts.

Base
Using A, cast on 5 sts,
leaving a length of yarn.
Row 1: P.
Row 2: K1, (m1, k1) to end (9 sts).
Row 3 and every alt row: P.
Row 4: K1, (m1, k1) to end (17 sts).
Row 6: K1, (m1, k2) to end (25 sts).
Row 8: K1, (m1, k3) to end (33 sts).
Row 10: K1, (m1, k4) to end (41 sts).
Row 11: P.
Row 12: K.
Cast off.

To make up
Sew in the cast-off ends of the petals,
leave a length of yarn at the cast-on edge.

Sew the seam of the circular base.
Block and press the pieces.

Sew the first petal to the last petal
on the inner section. Thread the

yarn through the cast-on edge
and gather. Secure, leaving
a length of yarn. With RS facing
up, wrap the yarn around the base
a little way up from the bottom
and secure.

Sew the first to the last petal of
the outer section. Thread the
yarn through the cast-on edge and
gather slightly into an open circle,
keeping the petals lying flat, to sit
on the circular base with a ¾in
(2cm) opening at the centre.
Do not sew this section onto
the base at this point.

Finish the inner section as the
outer section, leaving a small
opening. Place the inner piece into
the opening, so that the bottom
part below the wrapped yarn is
inside the opening. Pull to gather
and secure.

Pin the inner petals to each other,
overlapping slightly, and sew from
the front and back. This will pull
up this section so that it does not
lie flat. Place this so that it sits in
the opening of the outer petals,
and pin and secure from the back.

Pin the flower to the base with the
RS facing up on the base and sew
in place.

Knitting know-how

Use this section to find everything you need to know to get started, including tools, materials and clearly explained basic knitting techniques.

Tools and materials

The great thing about knitting is that it requires few tools. All you really need are some knitting needles and yarn, but it's helpful to have a few other things, as detailed below. Here are some of the most useful ones you'll need to make the projects. Most can be picked up easily and cheaply online or from local craft shops.

1. Knitting needles

These can be made from many different materials, depending on your preference and budget. Plastic needles tend to be a cheaper alternative and are light to use. You can also get wooden, bamboo and even metal needles. I have used straight and double-pointed needles for the projects.

2. Yarn

Yarn is usually sold wound into balls of a specific weight. The patterns for the designs in this book are worked in 4-ply, DK or Aran weight yarns. As small amounts are used, these are great stash-busting projects.

3. Scissors

Small scissors are best for cutting yarn.

4. Sewing needles and pins

You'll need a large tapestry needle with a large eye and a blunt tip for sewing up projects and weaving in loose ends. Using a blunt tip means you are less likely to split the yarn. You will also need a smaller needle and matching thread for sewing on flowers and adding details. Pins are required for blocking and holding pieces together.

5. Stitch holder

Stitch holders come in many sizes and hold anything up from one stitch. If you only need to hold a few stitches, you could use a safety pin instead.

6. Measuring tape or ruler

You'll need a measuring tape or ruler to measure the length of the project.

7. Crochet hook

Keep a crochet hook handy for picking up dropped stitches.

8. Miscellaneous

Many of the projects use florist's wire or wooden skewers for stiffening – this means they can be more easily displayed, too. You will need wire cutters to cut florist's wire to the right length. Polyester stuffing or cotton wool is used to give structure to various flowers; you will also need pieces of card and felt. Pieces of ribbon also come in handy for finishing some of the projects.

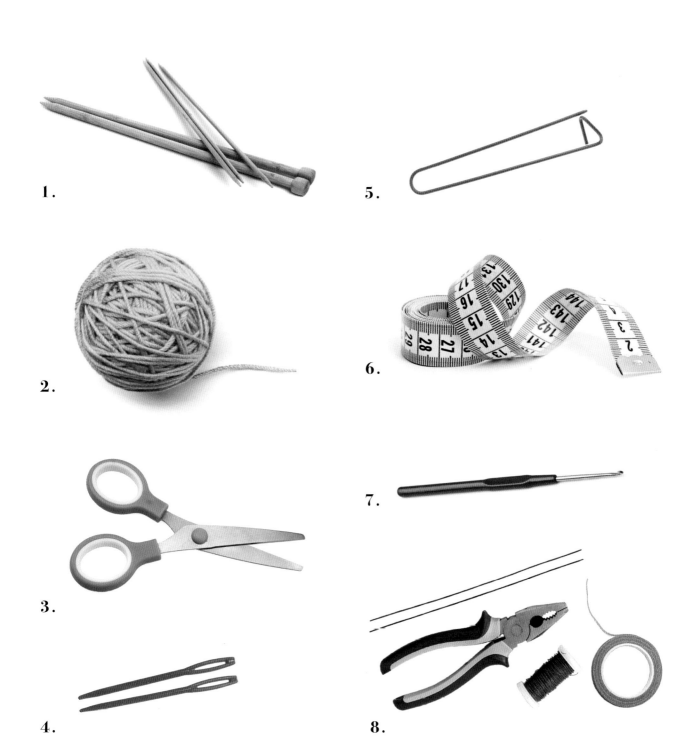

1.

2.

3.

4.

5.

6.

7.

8.

Basic techniques

Slipknot

1. Before you start to knit, you need to make the first loop on your needle. Create a loop a short distance from the end of the yarn. Take the yarn leading to the ball and pass a loop under and through the loop. Place this new loop over your knitting needle.

2. Pull both ends of the yarn to tighten the knot and shorten the loop. The loop (slipknot) should be loose enough so that you can insert the other knitting needle into it.

1.

2.

Casting on

There are many ways of casting on. Here are two of the most widely used ones. The two-needle cast-on method creates a firm edge while the thumb method creates an edge with more stretch that is less defined.

Two-needle method

1. Create a slipknot on the left-hand needle to form the first stitch; pull it taut but not too tight. Insert the right-hand needle into this stitch from front to back, so that it crosses behind the left-hand needle. Wrap the working yarn anticlockwise around the point of the right needle.

2. Pull the loop formed by wrapping the yarn through the original stitch forward and transfer the loop on to the tip of the left-hand needle. There will now be two stitches on the left needle.

3. Repeat steps 1 and 2, each time inserting the right needle into the last stitch made on the left needle. Continue until you have the correct number of stitches. For a firmer edge, cast on the first 2 sts as shown above. When casting on the third and subsequent sts, insert the needle between the cast-on sts on the left needle, wrap the yarn round and pull through to create a loop. Slide the loop on to the left needle. Repeat to end.

1.

2.

3.

Thumb method

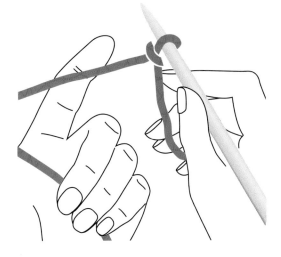

1. Leaving a long tail of yarn, make a slipknot on one knitting needle. You will need to estimate the length of the tail of yarn based on the width of the fabric you are going to create. As a rough guide, leave a long tail about three times this width.

2. Holding the needle in your right hand, wind the tail of yarn immediately next to the slipknot around your left thumb, from front to back. Insert the needle up through the loop of yarn on the thumb, then use your right forefinger to take the yarn over the point of the needle.

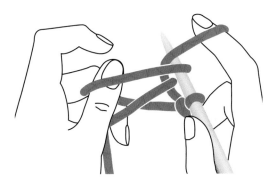

3. Pull a loop of yarn through to form the first stitch. Remove your left thumb from the yarn and tug on the yarn tail to secure the stitch.

Repeat the process until you have the required number of stitches on the needle.

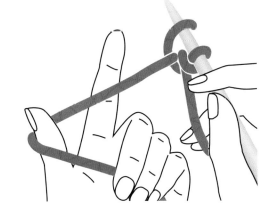

Basic stitches

Knit stitch

1. With the yarn at the back of the work, inset the tip of the right needle into the stitch on the left needle, upwards and from front to back; the right needle should cross behind the left needle. Wrap the yarn in a clockwise direction around the tip of the right needle.

2. Using the right needle, pull the loop of the wrapped yarn through the original stitch, creating a new stitch.

3. Slide the original stitch off the left-hand needle. The new stitch will be on the right needle.

Purl stitch

1. With the yarn at the front of the work, insert the tip of the right needle from right to left into the front loop of the first stitch; the right needle should be in front of the left needle. Wrap the yarn in a clockwise direction around the tip of the right needle.

2. Using the right needle, pull the loop backwards and allow the original stitch to slide off the left needle.

3. The new stitch will now be on the right needle.

1.

2.

1.

2.

3.

Garter stitch

Knit every row. This gives a thick, fully reversible fabric with ridges on both sides that don't curl.

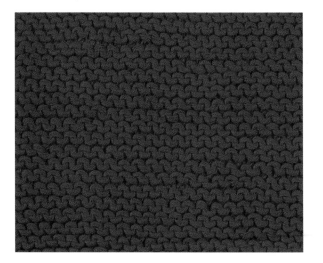

Stocking stitch

Knit on the right side and purl on the wrong side. This fabric is smooth on the right side and bumpy on the wrong side.

Increasing

Increases help to shape a piece of knitted fabric. Here are some of the most common ways to increase stitches.

Working into the same stitch twice

The instruction kfb and pfb indicate that you need to work into the same stitch twice.

On a knit row:
Knit the next stitch but, before slipping it off the left needle, insert the right needle into the back loop and knit again.

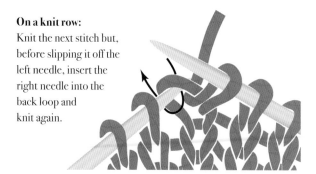

On a purl row:
Purl the next stitch but, before slipping it off the needle, insert the needle into the back loop and purl again.

Make a stitch

The instruction M1 indicates that you should create a new stitch in between two stitches. Having knitted or purled a stitch, use the tip of the right-hand needle to lift the strand of yarn lying in front of and just below the next stitch. Place it on the left-hand needle, then knit or purl into the back of this loop.

Decreasing

Knit two stitches together [k2tog or p2tog]

Decreases can be used for shaping your knitting.

1. Insert the right needle into the next two stitches instead of just one.

2. Knit (or purl) them together as if they were one stitch.

1.

2.

Picking up dropped stitches

If you have dropped a stitch and not noticed, it can form a ladder running in a line below the place where it was dropped. In this case, use a crochet hook to solve the problem. Working from the front, identify the stitch loop at the base of the ladder, pick up the strand of yarn immediately above and pull it through the stitch loop to form a new stitch on that row. Repeat this process, working upwards until you reach the row you are currently working on.

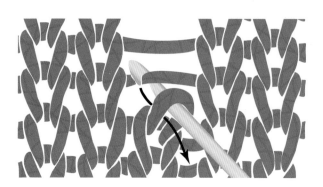

Joining in new yarns and changing colours

Wherever possible, join in a new yarn at the beginning of a row. Leave a tail of yarn and loosely knot the tails of the new and old yarns together. If you have to join in a new yarn in the middle of a row, simply pick up the new yarn, leaving a tail, and carry on knitting. Once you have completed a few rows, darn in the tails of the new and old yarns neatly at the back of the work.

Intarsia

Blocks of colour are worked using the intarsia technique. The front petals in the pansy project (see page 76) are created in this way. Twist the two different yarns together at the back of the work with each colour change to prevent holes appearing. Once finished, weave in ends at the back of the work.

Casting off

There are two basic ways to cast off a stitch: one is knitwise and the other purlwise. You should, as a general rule, cast off in pattern: this means that you should cast off a knit stitch knitwise and a purl stitch purlwise.

Casting off knitwise

1. Knit the first two stitches. Using the tip of the left needle, lift the first stitch over the second and off the right needle.

2. Knit the next stitch and lift the previous stitch over this stitch and off the right-hand needle. Repeat until all stitches have been cast off.

1.

2.

Casting off purlwise

Follow the instructions for casting off knitwise but purl the stitches.

I-cord

This useful stitch technique creates a rounded cord like a tube of knitting.

1. Using double-pointed needles, cast on the number of stitches required (usually 2, 3, 4 or 5, depending on the thickness you want).

2. Knit one row. Do not turn the work.

3. Slide the stitches from one end of the needle to the other.

4. Bring the yarn behind the work and knit another row. Repeat until the I-cord is the desired length.

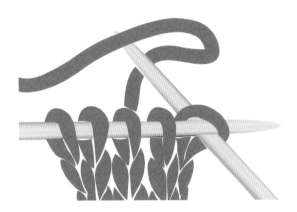

Finishing touches

Darning in loose ends

Every piece of knitting will have at least two loose ends: one on the corner of the cast-on edge and one at the end of the cast-off edge. If you have joined in more yarn at any stage, you will also have other ends to deal with. These can be used for sewing up: leave long tails if you know these will be used for this purpose. Otherwise, you need to weave in these ends. Thread each one in turn through a tapestry needle and weave it vertically or horizontally down the side of the work or through a row of stitches on the wrong side.

Blocking and pressing

This describes the process of shaping finished pieces of knitting to even out the stitches.

Wet blocking

Dampen the pieces, either by spraying with water or by immersing in water. Gently squeeze out any excess water, then place on a suitable surface such as a board covered with a cloth and use pins to hold the edges in place. Leave to dry.

Pressing

Place the knitted piece on a suitable surface, lay a clean, damp cloth on top, and gently press with an iron on a wool stetting. Gently stretch out the knitting to the desired measurements. Do not place the iron directly on to the knitted piece and be very careful if your yarn has acrylic fibres as these will melt with heat!

Sewing up

Use mattress stitch to sew up the flowers. You will need a large tapestry needle with a blunt tip – using a blunt tip means that you are less likely to split the yarn.

1. Place the two pieces to be joined right side up and with the edges touching. Thread a tapestry needle with a loose end of yarn and push the needle through the centre of the first stitch on one of the pieces, then in and out through the centres of two stitches on the opposite piece.

2. Now take the needle back over to the first piece, insert it where it previously came out and bring it out through the centre of the next stitch along. Repeat the process, alternating sides and inserting the needle under single stitches each time. After a few rows, pull on the yarn to bring the edges together, then continue until the two pieces are joined. The seam should be almost invisible.

Embroidery

To start your embroidery invisibly, tie a knot at the end of the yarn. Bring the needle through the back of the work, coming up through the front to begin the embroidery. The knot should be hidden at the back of the knitting. To fasten off invisibly, sew a few stitches back and forth through the work, inserting the needle where the yarn comes out.

Chain stitch

Bring the needle up through your work to start the first stitch and hold down the thread with the left thumb. Now insert the needle in the same place and bring the point out a short distance away. Keeping the working thread under the needle point, pull the loop of thread to form a chain.

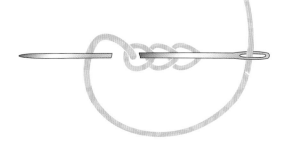

Straight stitch

Come up to start the embroidery at one end of the stitch then go back down at the end of the stitch, coming up in a different place to start the next stitch.

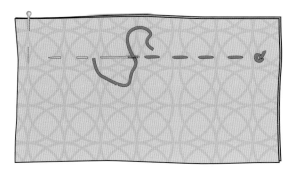

French knot

Bring your needle up through the fabric and then wrap your thread around the needle three times. Then insert the needle back into the fabric very close to where it emerged.

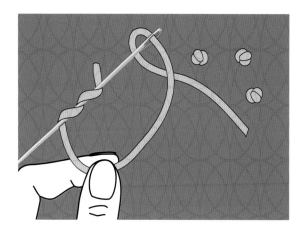

Abbreviations

alt	alternate		**patt**	pattern
beg	beginning		**p2tog**	purl two stitches together
cm	centimetre(s)		**psso**	pass slipped stitch over
cont	continue		**rem**	remaining
dec	decrease		**rep**	repeat
DK	double knitting		**RS**	right side
dpn	double-pointed needle		**sl**	slip
folls	follows		**st(s)**	stitch(es)
inc	increase by working into the front, then the back of the stitch		**st st**	stocking stitch
k	knit		**WS**	wrong side
kfb	knit into the front and back of the next stitch to increase		**yo**	take yarn over point of right-hand needle
k2tog	knit two stitches together			
m1	make one stitch: pick up the horizontal strand lying between the stitch just worked and the next stitch, and knit it			
m1p	make one stitch: pick up the horizontal strand lying between the stitch just worked and the next stitch, and purl it			
p	purl			

Conversions

UK/US yarn weights

UK	US
4-ply	Sport
DK (double knitting)	Light worsted

Knitting needle sizes

UK	METRIC	US
10	3.25	3
9	3.75	5

Index

First published 2024 by
Guild of Master Craftsman Publications Ltd
Castle Place, 166 High Street, Lewes, East Sussex BN7 1XU, UK

ISBN 978 1 78494 677 7

Publisher: Jonathan Bailey
Production: Jim Bulley
Senior Project Editor: Sara Harper
Design Manager: Robin Shields
Design and illustration: Emily Hurlock
Photography: Andrew Perris
Stylist: Anna Stevens

Colour origination by GMC Reprographics
Printed and bound in China

To order a book, contact:
GMC Publications Ltd
Castle Place, 166 High Street,
Lewes, East Sussex BN7 1XU, UK
Tel: +44(0)1273 488005
www.gmcbooks.com